I use a 'Sharpie' paint pen' in Yellow or White to draw right on the foam so I can easily tell where the die is located.

It is easy to selectively cut pieces by positioning a section of fabric over a specific die. The 'paint pen' outline really helps.

For appliques, I usually secure fusible web to the back of fabrics before I die cut the shapes. Or you can cut first then fuse.

It is easy to 'fussy cut' pieces after you die cut the master shape. This is good for bodies and to make layers.

Cut a 'snowflake' of butterflies or shapes, by folding a square twice to make a smaller square. Place both folds just 'inside' the cut lines so they stay together when cut.

Holidays - pages 4 - 5

Quilts, Pots and Floorcloth - pages 6 - 8

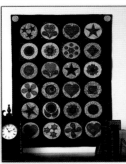

Quilts and Place Mats - pages 9 - 43 - 44

Quilts and Pillows
pages 45 - 47

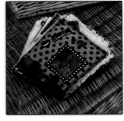

Place Mats, Table Runner, Pillow and Quilt - pages 48 - 49

GO!™

All die designs
©1990-2010 by
AccuQuilt.
AccuQuilt® and GO!™
are trademarks
of AccuQuilt.

Scrapbook - page 10
Totes - page 50
Borders Quilt - page 51

Festive Aprons

sewn by Kayleen Allen
The joys of the holidays spring from times shared so invite your family into the kitchen to participate in the pleasures of preparing the feast or just have fun making cookies.

These festive aprons will keep the holiday dresses neat and tidy, so be sure to keep a few on hand. With these easy sewing techniques and speedy appliques, you'll be able to make an apron for every child and adult.

instructions on page 14

Holiday Stockings

sewn by Ja Peck

The stockings were hung by the chimney with care... but since we didn't have a fireplace, we set them near the chair.

Nothing says 'Happy Christmas' like stockings. They represent the promise of sugar plum dreams and children nestled snugly in their beds.

Capture the romance of the season with a personal collection of handmade stockings.

instructions on page 15

Seasonal Towels

applique by Ja Peck

For those of us who love to decorate, these towels will accent your kitchen or buffet table beautifully with favorite seasonal motifs.

Accu-Cut makes these appliques easy, so you'll have time to bedeck towels for your friends. These make fabulous fast gifts!

instructions on page 15

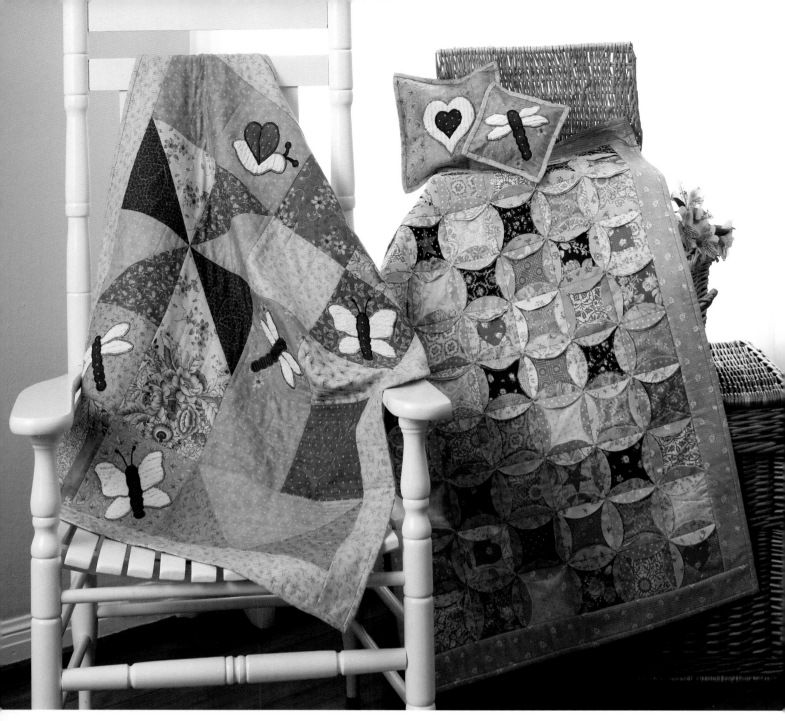

Summer Breeze Quilt and Mini Pillows

sewn by Edna Summers

Dragonflies drift lazily on an afternoon breeze as butterflies dance among the flowers on this pastel mix of yellows and greens.

Capture the essence of those long, lazy summer afternoons by relaxing with this wonderful project in your sewing room.

Use leftover fabrics and the same motifs as the Summer Breeze quilt to make small accent pillows. These are pretty accents for a bedroom dresser and they are also perfect for a doll cradle.

instructions on page 38

Reversible Cathedral Windows

sewn by Janice Irick

Here's a quilt that, upon closer inspection, ignites your curiosity until you demand to know 'how did they do that great look?'

Once you learn this fabulous layering technique, you will find it difficult to stop with a small quilt. This is going to be a quilt show favorite, and it's reversible! The charming back is created as you sew.

instructions on page 36

Summer Cottage in the Mountains

sewn by Edna Summers

Experience a summer in Provence without leaving your sewing room. Summer Cottage captures the splendor of a field of flowers in an exceptionally beautiful part of France.

You'll love the construction method of 'sew first, cut second' as a time saving technique for making these charming smountains.

instructions on pages 34 - 35

Toybox Critters Quilt

pieced by
Donna Perrotta

quilted by
Sue Needle

Like Christopher Robin, your child will spend hours inventing adventurous tales of Hooty Owl, Squeeky Mouse, Teddy Bear, Betty Butterfly, Lady Bug, Charlie Caterpillar, and Bunny Rabbit.

This creative quilt presents these friends like the drawings in a children's book, ready for your journey of the imagination.

instructions on pages 28 - 29

No-Sew Flower Pots and Floor Cloth

made by
Donna Perrotta

Use the same fabrics and motifs from your quilt to create a coordinating rug with this sturdy no-sew technique.

This floor mat will withstand hours of imaginative play and wipes clean with a damp cloth.

instructions on page 29

Dance of the Sunflowers

pieced by Donna Perrotta
quilted by Sue Needle

Dance of the Sunflowers crosses the line from quilt to art for several reasons. The astounding simplistic beauty of flowing stems and flower heads that float effortlessly lighten even the most heavily burdened soul.

The beautifully pieced background creates a softly blended light and dark watercolor effect that supports the subject without interfering, so the flowers present each viewer with a uniquely private performance.

instructions on page 31

Timeless Fabric Scrapbook

made by Suzanne Sparks

This book tells a personal story of a life's journey with its wisdom, insights, purpose and dreams.

Fabric offers a flexibility and texture that is different from the usual book. More importantly, the journaling gives one a glimpse into the artist's soul with handwritten expressions of love for family, friendship, and the search for meaning in life.

When books like these are made with authentic honesty, they become the timeless family treasures through which we are not only remembered, but known and understood.

One of my favorite sayings is "Just when I thought life was over, I became a butterfly," sighed the caterpillar.

The intriguing cover uses tulle netting to make a window, a technique commonly found in altered paper books. Each of the ten pages is numbered with a fabric applique. You can also add words, numbers, sayings and journaling with embroidery or with a Black permanent marker.

It is fun to attach metal trinkets, charms and embellishments by pinning, clipping, or sewing them in place.

Prairie point triangle tabs make the pages easy to turn while other pages sport decorative fringe edges. There are half-pages embedded within, providing extra space for artful expression.

This book is brimming with texture and meaningful expressions.

instructions on page 11

Fabric Scrapbook

photo is on page 10

SIZE: 6½" x 7"

YARDAGE:

We used a *Moda* "Authentic" by Sweetwater,
we purchased 1 'Layer Cake' collection
of 10" x 10" squares or use leftover fabrics

16 squares	OR	1⅙ yards Ivory
12 squares	OR	⅞ yard Black
7 squares	OR	⅝ yard Light Green
3 squares	OR	⅓ yard Red
2 squares	OR	⅓ yard Tan

10" x 15" scrap of Black tulle
10" x 15" scrap of White lace
4" x 4" scrap of White chenille
1 yard cotton drill fabric
Advantus idea-ology trinkets available from
Product Performers at www.productperformers.com
Sewing machine, needle, thread
Assorted charms,
Scraps of ribbon & lace
6 yards of Lightweight fusible interfacing
4 yards of Fusible web
Black permanent marker
AccuQuilt® GO!™ Fabric Cutter (#55100),
(refer to pages 12-13 for dies)
GO! die #55000 Square 6½" (full pages and half pages)
GO! die #55005 Rectangle (spines)
Assorted dies for embellishments:
GO! die #55021 Square 2½" (windows)
GO! die #55012 Circles 2", 3", 5"
GO! die #55028 Stars 2", 3", 4"
GO! die #55029 Hearts 2", 3", 4"
GO! die #55030 Critters - bee, butterfly, dragonfly

PREPARATION FOR APPLIQUES:
Press fusible web onto the back of all pieces except tulle
before cutting. Die cut assorted pieces as desired.

PREPARING THE PAGES, COVER & SPINE:
Use the following fabrics for pages, spines and cover:
Black, Ivory, Light Green, Tan
Use Ivory drill fabric (canvas) between the pages for fringed
texture along the edges of the pages.

DIECUT THE PAGES, COVER & SPINE:
Pages - Die cut 6½" x 6½" squares from assorted fabrics.
Half Pages - Die cut 6½" x 6½" squares then fold in half.
Spines - Die cut 3½" x 6½" strips for spine pieces.
Tabs - Die cut 3½" x 3½" squares for tabs.

TIPS FOR PAGES, COVER & SPINE:
Save all leftover scraps for applique pieces and details.
Fuse interfacing to the wrong side of each page and half page.
Use Ivory drill fabric (frayed on the edges) inside of pages to
get a great texture around the edges.
Cut a window through a page. Stitch around the edge.
Use tulle netting in windows, and as an overlay applique.
Sew a ribbon around the page edges or window edge.
Sew lace edging to the pages.

Prairie Points for Page Tabs
1. Fold a 3½" square in half.
2. Fold fabric again to form a triangle. Press.

Full page   folded edge   Half page   Double page

MAKING THE PAGES:
Full Pages:
1. For each full page, place 2 pages together (with the right side out)
sandwiching the interfacing between them.
2. Insert a Prairie Point tab somewhere on the outside edge. Pin in place.
3. Sew around the edges of each page.
4. Decorate each page as desired - use appliques, cut out windows, buttons,
lace, tulle, ribbon, trinkets, etc.
TIP;: Applique numbers on pages or embroider numbers with Black floss.

Half Pages:
1. Fold 1 full page in half (with right side out) sandwiching the interfacing inside.
2. .Sew around the edges of each page.
3. Decorate each page as desired - use appliques, buttons, lace, tulle, ribbon, etc.

Double Pages:
1. Make 1 full page and 1 half page.
2. Stack the half page on top of the full page.
3. Stitch along the edge.

Full page
Half page
or
Double page

Spine

Full page
Half page
or
Double page

ASSEMBLE EACH SET OF PAGES:
1. Choose pairs of facing pages (full, half or double) and arrange them on a table.
2. Choose 2 spine strips for the center (one for the top and one for the bottom).
3. Pin the spine in place.
4. Topstitch the spine strip on all sides to hold the pages in place.

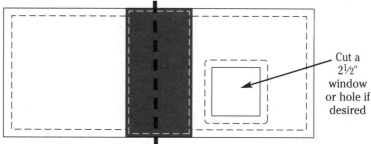

Cut a 2½" window or hole if desired

ASSEMBLE THE BOOK:
1. Stack sets of pages on top of each other (I had a total of 9 sets of pages.
2. Hand stitch through all layers along the center of the spines with Black floss
using a Running Stitch to hold the book together.
3. Embellish and decorate the book as desired. Journal some words and thoughts.

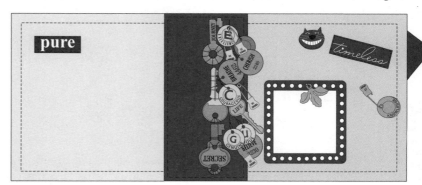

accuquilt GO!
better cuts make better quilts

Mix & Match Quilt Dies for Piecing

Enlarge at 400% to use as templates.

Pictured on these pages are the AccuQuilt® GO!™ shapes and die descriptions that we used to create all the quilts in this book.

All dies are pictured at 25% of actual size.

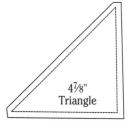

3½"
Triangle

GO! die #55009
Half Square -
3" Finished Triangle
Includes seam allowance.

4⅞"
Triangle

GO! die #55002
Triangle - 4⅞"
Includes seam allowance.

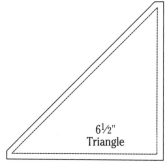

6½"
Triangle

GO! die #55001
Triangle - 6½" (6" finished)
Includes seam allowance.

3½"
Square

GO! die #55006
Square - 3½" (3" finished)
Includes seam allowance.

4¾"
Square

GO! die #55019
Square - 4¾" (4" finished)
Includes seam allowance.
(use on point)

6½"
Square

GO! die #55000
Square - 6½" (6" finished)
Includes seam allowance.

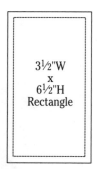

5"W x 6"H
Triangle -
Isosceles

GO! die #55016
Triangle - Isosceles - 5"W x 6"H
Includes seam allowance.

3½"W
x
6½"H
Rectangle

GO! die #55005
Rectangle - 3½"W x 6½"H
(3"W x 6"H finished)
Includes seam allowance.

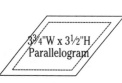

3¾"W x 3½"H
Parallelogram

GO! die #55004
Parallelogram - 3¾"W x 3½"H
Includes seam allowance.

6½" Tumbler

GO! die #55020
Tumbler - 6½"
Includes seam allowance.

fold fabric on one end
to cut 2½" x 44" Strips

GO! die #55017
Strip Cutter - 2½" (2" finished strips)
Includes seam allowance.

2½"
Triangle

2½"
Square

4½" Square

GO! die #55021
Die for 3 shapes
2½" Square (2" finished) - 2½" Triangle (2" finished) - 4½" Square 4" finished)
Includes seam allowance.

accuquilt GO!
better cuts make better quilts®

Mix & Match Quilt Dies for Applique
Enlarge at 400% to use as templates.

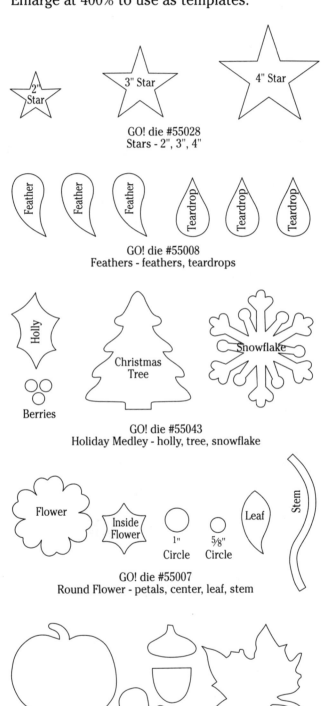

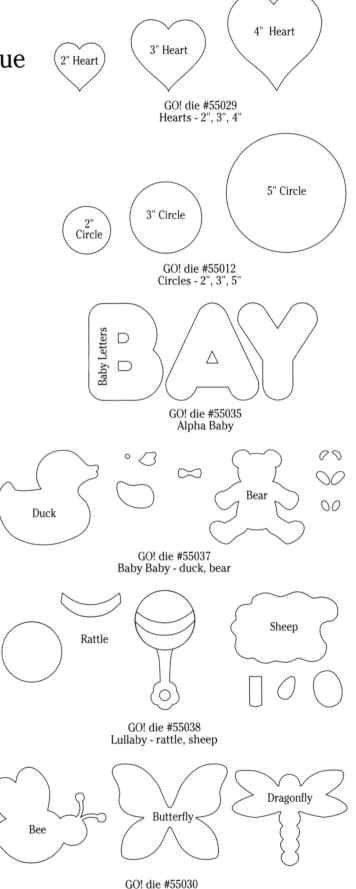

GO! die #55028
Stars - 2", 3", 4"

GO! die #55008
Feathers - feathers, teardrops

GO! die #55043
Holiday Medley - holly, tree, snowflake

GO! die #55007
Round Flower - petals, center, leaf, stem

GO! die #55041
Fall Medley - pumpkin, leaf, acorn, large leaf

GO! die #55029
Hearts - 2", 3", 4"

GO! die #55012
Circles - 2", 3", 5"

GO! die #55035
Alpha Baby

GO! die #55037
Baby Baby - duck, bear

GO! die #55038
Lullaby - rattle, sheep

GO! die #55030
Critters - bee, butterfly, dragonfly

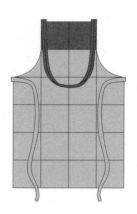

Child Apron Assembly Diagram

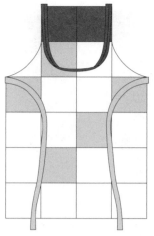

Adab Apron Assembly Diagram

Child Apron

Adult Apron

Festive Aprons

photo on page 4
SIZE: Adult: 24" x 36"
Child: 12" x 18"

YARDAGE:
We used a *Moda* "Love U" by Deb Strain
we purchased 1 'Layer Cake' collection
of 10" x 10" squares or use leftover fabrics

15 squares	OR	⅓ yard White prints (adult)
5 squares	OR	⅝ yard Yellow prints (adult)
5 squares	OR	⅝ yard Pink prints (child)

Applique Fabric:
20" x 28" of Red dots (adult and child)
12" x 28" of Green dots (adult and child)

Backing   Purchase ⅜ yd for Child Apron, ¾ yard for Adult
Sewing machine, needle, thread
2 yards of Fusible web
4 yards of lightweight iron-on interfacing
AccuQuilt® GO!™ Fabric Cutter (#55100),
(refer to pages 12-13 for dies)
GO! die #55006 Square $3\frac{1}{2}$" (3" finished)
GO! die #55000 Square $6\frac{1}{2}$" (6" finished)
GO! die #55043 Holiday Medley - holly, tree, snowflake

PREPARATION FOR BLOCKS:
If you use 10" squares, cut a 3" strip off each square.
Set the 3" strips aside for making the waist straps.
Die cut all pieces as listed below.

Color	**#55006 Square $3\frac{1}{2}$"**
Pink	20 for Child Apron
Red Dot	2 for Child Apron

Color	**#55000 Square $6\frac{1}{2}$"**
White	15 for Adult Apron
Yellow	5 for Adult Apron
Red Dot	2 for Adult Apron

PREPARATION FOR APPLIQUES:
Press fusible web onto the back of all pieces before cutting.
Die cut all pieces as listed below).

For Child Apron:

Color	**#55043 Holiday Medley**
Red dot	1 Tree, 12 Berries
Green dot	1 Tree, 6 Berries, 8 Holly

For Adult Apron:

Color	**#55043 Holiday Medley**
Red dot	1 Tree, 1 Snowflake, 19 Berries
Green dot	2 Trees, 5 Berries, 15 Holly

ASSEMBLY FOR EACH APRON:
Note: All sizes of aprons are assembled in the same manner.
The child apron uses $3\frac{1}{2}$" squares.
The adult apron uses $6\frac{1}{2}$" squares.
To make a teen apron use $4\frac{1}{2}$" squares.

ASSEMBLY FOR ALL APRONS:
Arrange all pieces on a work surface or table.
Sew 4 rows of 4 blocks together. Press.
Sew 2 Red dot squares to the center top.
Trim outer squares on row 2 in a curve as shown.
Applique as desired.
Using apron as a pattern, cut out a lining fabric.

ADD STRIPS FOR WAIST AND NECK:
Sew strips for apron waist straps end to end to make 2 straps, 20" for child and 30" for adult). With right sides together, fold strips lengthwise then sew along the edge and 1 end. Turn right side out. Position at armholes and sew to apron.
Cut a Red dot neck strap for each apron: $2\frac{1}{2}$" x 20" for child, $2\frac{1}{2}$" x 28" for adult. With right sides together, fold lengthwise and sew the edge. Position at neck and sew to apron.

ADD LINING:
With right sides together, sew the lining to the apron, leaving a 6" opening for turning. Turn right side out. Hand stitch the opening closed. Press.

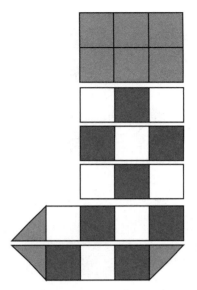

Sew square patches and triangles together.

Checkerboard Stocking

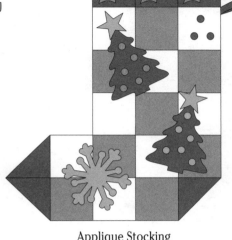

Applique Stocking

Holiday Stockings

photo on page 5
SIZE: 14" x17$\frac{1}{2}$"

YARDAGE:
We used assorted leftover fabrics:
   $\frac{1}{3}$ yard White stripe
   $\frac{1}{3}$ yard Red stripe
   $\frac{1}{3}$ yard Green
   5" x 14" scrap of Red print
   3" x 5" scrap of Yellow
   5" x 10" scrap of Gold
   5" x 8" scrap of Green dot
Sewing machine, needle, thread
10" Red $\frac{1}{2}$" wide rick rack
1 yard of Fusible web (for Applique stocking)
2 yards of lightweight iron-on interfacing
AccuQuilt® GO!™ Fabric Cutter (#55100),
      (refer to pages 12-13 for dies)
   GO! die #55006 Square 3$\frac{1}{2}$" (3" finished)
   GO! die #55009 Half Square Triangle (3" finished)
   GO! die #55043 Holiday Medley - holly, tree, snowflake
   GO! die #55028 Stars - 2", 3", 4"

PREPARATION FOR BLOCKS:
Die cut all pieces as listed below.

Color	#55006 Square 3$\frac{1}{2}$"
Green stripe	14
White stripe	16
Red solid	14

Color	#55009 Half Square Triangle
Green stripe	3
Red solid	3

PREPARATION FOR APPLIQUES:
Press fusible web onto the back of all
   pieces before cutting.
Die cut all pieces as listed below.

Color	#55043 Seasonal
Gold	1 Snowflake, 6 Berries
Green dot	6 Berries, 3 Holly
Red	2 Trees, 3 Berries

Color	#55028 Stars
Yellow	2 Stars - 2"

CUT PIECES:
   Cut 2 scraps 1" x 8" for the hangers.
ASSEMBLY:
   Arrange all pieces on a work surface.
   Sew square patches and triangles
      together. Press.
   Press iron-on interfacing on the back.
   Sew rick rack on Checkerboard stocking.
   Embroider a name with 6 ply floss if desired.
   Applique Green stocking as desired.
   Use the stocking as a pattern to cut out
      2 linings & 1 backing for each stocking.
   Layer backing, front, lining, lining.
      with right sides together.
      Sew hanger strip into a tube.
   Position hanger in the seam.
   Sew around stocking leaving the top open.
   Turn stocking right side out.
   Turn under the top edge and hem by hand.

Seasonal Towels

photo on page 5
SIZE: 21" x 28"

YARDAGE:
We used assorted leftover fabrics:
   8" x 12" scrap of White
   16" x 16" scrap of Green
   12" x 16" scrap of Red
   3" x 10" scrap of Yellow
   8" x 8" scrap of Lace
Sewing machine, needle, thread
3 homespun fabric kitchen towels, each 21" x 28"
24" Red $\frac{1}{2}$" wide rick rack
1 yard of Fusible web
AccuQuilt® GO!™ Fabric Cutter (#55100),
      (refer to pages 12-13 for dies)
   GO! die #55043 Holiday Medley - holly, tree, snowflake
   GO! die #55028 Stars - 2", 3", 4"

PREPARATION FOR APPLIQUES:
Press fusible web onto the back of all
   pieces before cutting.

Trees and Holly

Trees

Snowflake

Die cut all pieces as listed below.

Color	#55043 Seasonal
White	2 Snowflakes, 4 Berries
Lace	1 Snowflake, 5 Berries
Green	6 Trees, 16 Berries, 7 Holly
Red	2 Trees, 42 Berries, 1 Snowflake

Color	#55028 Stars
Yellow	4 Stars 2"

ASSEMBLY:
   Arrange all pieces on a work surface.
   Applique as desired.
   Sew rick rack to the bottom of one towel.

Dragonfly and Butterfly Place Mat Assembly

TIP: If desired, die-cut the butterfly or dragonfly from a second color then fussy-cut the body to add a layer to your applique.

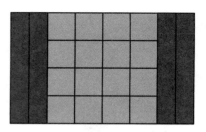

Basic Assembly Diagram for All Place Mats

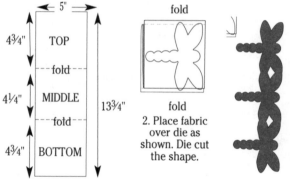

Dragonfly Place Mat Assembly

1. Cut a fabric strip 5" x 13¾". Accordion fold it.

fold

2. Place fabric over die as shown. Die cut the shape.

3. Unfold to reveal 3 connected dragonflies.

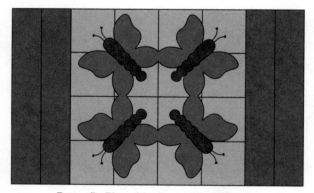

Butterfly Place Mat Assembly Diagram

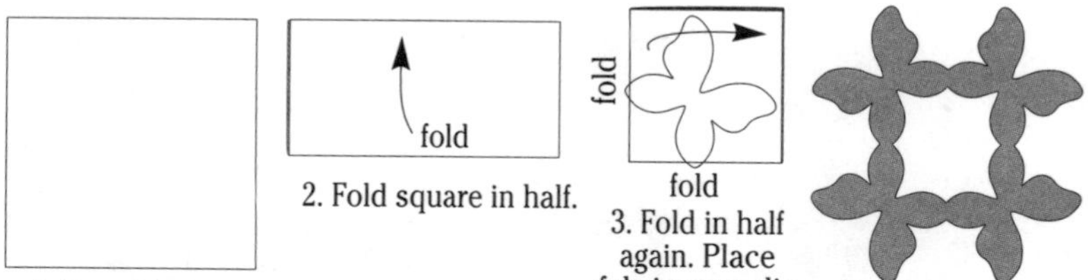

1. Cut a fabric square 12" x 12".

2. Fold square in half.

3. Fold in half again. Place fabric over die edges at folds. Die cut shape.

4. Unfold fabric to reveal 4 connected butterflies.

Summer's Buzz Place Mats

photo on page 44
SIZE: 12" x 20"

YARDAGE FOR 3 PLACE MATS:
We used a *Moda* "Civil War Homefront" by Barbara Brackman, we purchased 1 'Layer Cake' collection of 10" x 10" squares or use leftover fabrics

4 squares	OR	⅓ yard Mauve
2 squares	OR	⅓ yard Cranberry
6 squares	OR	⅝ yard Light Brown
2 squares	OR	⅓ yard Blue
4 squares	OR	⅓ yard Tan
1 square	OR	10" x 10" scrap of Black

Appliques & Binding	Purchase ⅞ yard of Dark Red print
Backing	Purchase ⅝ yard
Batting	Purchase 21" x 39"

Sewing machine, needle, thread
2 yards of Fusible web
AccuQuilt® GO!™ Fabric Cutter (#55100), (refer to pages 12-13 for dies)
    GO! die #55006 Square 3½" (3" finished)
    GO! die #55030 Critters
    GO! die #55017 Strip Cutter 2½" (2" finished)

SORTING:

Place Mat	Center	Sides
1.	Tan	Light Brown
2.	Mauve	Cranberry
3.	Light Brown	Blue

PREPARATION FOR BLOCKS:
Die cut all pieces as listed below.

Color	#55006 Square 3½"
Tan	16
Mauve	16
Light Brown	16

Color	#55017 Strip Cutter 2½"
Light Brown	6 strips 2½" x 10"
Cranberry	6 strips 2½" x 10"
Blue	6 strips 2½" x 10"

PREPARATION FOR APPLIQUES:
Press fusible web onto the back of all pieces before cutting.
Die cut all pieces as listed below.

Color	#55030 Critters
Dark Red print 12" square 5" x 13¾" strip	1 Butterfly, 1 Dragonfly, 1 set of 4 Butterflies (see diagram) 1 set of 3 Dragonflies (see diagram)
Black	9 Dragonfly bodies

ASSEMBLY:
Arrange all pieces on a work surface or table.
For each place mat, sew squares together in 4 rows, 4 squares per row. Press.
Sew 4 strips 2½" x 12½" for each place mat. Press.
Sew 2 strips to each side of each place mat. Press.
Applique as desired.

FINISHING:
Quilting: See Basic Instructions.
Binding: For each place mat, sew 2½" strips together end to end to equal 74". See Binding Instructions on page 19.

Sampler Blocks
Place Mats, Table Runners, Quilts

photo on page 48
SIZE: Runner: 12" x 42", Place Mat: 12" x 18"
YARDAGE:
We used *Moda* Marbles and "Civil War Homefront" by Barbara Brackman.

   we purchased 1 'Layer Cake' collection of 10" x 10" squares or use leftover fabrics
$1\frac{1}{8}$ yard of Black for blocks and binding
$\frac{5}{8}$ yard Tan
$\frac{1}{2}$ yard Red
Backing   Purchase $1\frac{1}{8}$ yard
Batting   Purchase 13" x 43" for runner
          Purchase 13" x 19" for mat
Sewing machine, needle, thread
AccuQuilt® GO!™ Fabric Cutter (#55100),
   (refer to pages 12-13 for dies)
   GO! die #55000 Square $6\frac{1}{2}$" (6" finished)
   GO! die #55019 Square on point $4\frac{3}{4}$" (4")
   GO! die #55021 Square $2\frac{1}{2}$" (2" finished)
   GO! die #55006 Square $3\frac{1}{2}$" (3" finished)
   GO! die #55005 Rectangle $3\frac{1}{2}$" x $6\frac{1}{2}$" (3" x 6")
   GO! die #55001 Triangle $6\frac{1}{2}$" (6" finished)
   GO! die #55009 Triangle $3\frac{1}{2}$" (3" finished)
   GO! die #55017 Strip Cutter $2\frac{1}{2}$" (2" finished)

PREPARATION FOR BLOCKS:
Die cut all pieces as listed below.

Block #	#55009 Triangle $3\frac{1}{2}$"
1	4 Black, 4 Tan
2	4 Black, 4 Tan
3	4 Black, 4 Tan
4	4 Black
6	2 Black, 2 Tan
Block #	**#55019 Square on point**
4	1 Tan
Block #	**#55001 Triangle $6\frac{1}{2}$"**
5	1 Black, 1 Tan
11	10 Red print
Block #	**#55005 Rectangle $3\frac{1}{2}$" x $6\frac{1}{2}$"**
6	1 Tan
10	1 Black, 1 Tan
Block #	**#55021 Square $2\frac{1}{2}$"**
7	5 Black, 4 Tan
9	5 Black, 4 Tan
Block #	**#55006 Square $3\frac{1}{2}$"**
8	2 Black, 2 Tan

PREPARATION FOR BINDING:

Color	#55017 Strip Cutter $2\frac{1}{2}$"
Black	5 strips $2\frac{1}{2}$" x 42"
	(3 for runner, 2 for mat)

ASSEMBLY:
   Sew 1 each of Blocks 1-10.
      Refer to diagrams for block construction.
   Table Runner:
   Sew 7 rows of 2 blocks per row. Press.
      Sew the rows together. Press.
   Place Mat:
   Sew 2 rows of 3 blocks per row. Press.
      Sew the rows together. Press.

FINISHING:
Quilting:
   See Basic Instructions.
Binding:
   See Binding Instructions on page 19.
Table Runner:
   Sew strips together end to end to equal 118".
Place Mat:
   Sew strips together end to end to equal 70".

'Mix and Match' Blocks

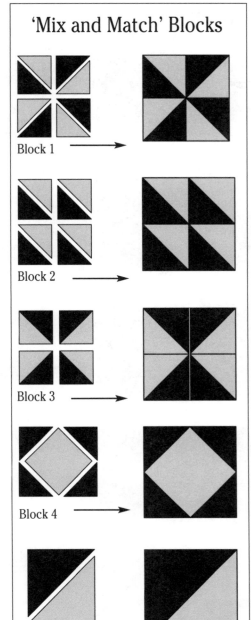

Block 1
Block 2
Block 3
Block 4
Block 5

'Mix and Match' Blocks

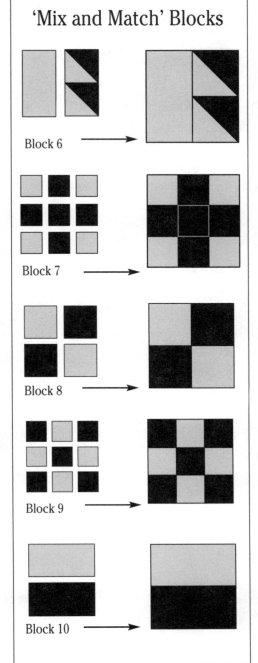

Block 6
Block 7
Block 8
Block 9
Block 10

Basic Square

Block 11

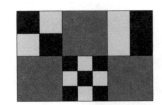

Place Mat Assembly Diagram

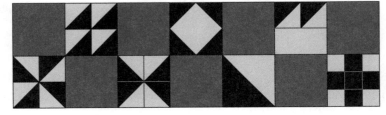

Table Runner Assembly Diagram

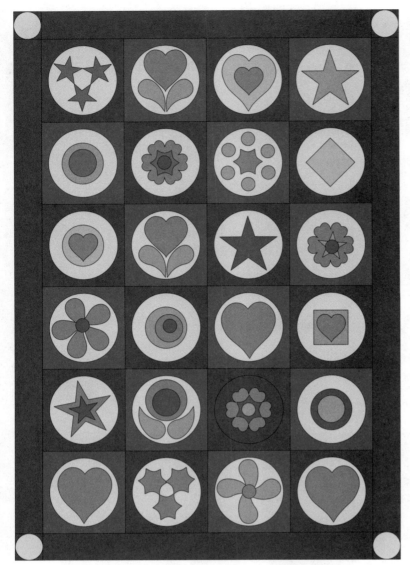

Pennsylvania Dutch Quilt Assembly Diagram

Pennsylvania Dutch Quilt

photo on page 45
SIZE: 28" x 40"

YARDAGE:
We used a *Moda* "Blessings" by Brannock & Patek,
    we purchased 1 'Layer Cake' collection
      of 10" x 10" squares or use leftover fabrics

8 squares	OR	$\frac{5}{8}$ yard Tan
4 squares	OR	$\frac{1}{3}$ yard Red
3 squares	OR	$\frac{1}{3}$ yard Green
2 squares	OR	10" x 20" scrap of Blue
1 squares	OR	10" x 10" scrap of Brown

$\frac{2}{3}$ yard Black print

Blocks, Border & Binding	Purchase $1\frac{1}{3}$ yards Black
Backing	Purchase $1\frac{3}{8}$ yards
Batting	Purchase 36" x 48"

Sewing machine, needle, thread
4 yards of Fusible web
6 yards of lightweight iron-on interfacing
AccuQuilt® GO!™ Fabric Cutter (#55100),
    (refer to pages 12-13 for dies)
    GO! die #55000 Square $6\frac{1}{2}$" (6" finished)
    GO! die #55021 Square $2\frac{1}{2}$" (2" finished)
    GO! die #55012 Circles 2"-3"-5"
    GO! die #55028 Stars 2"-3"-4"
    GO! die #55007 Round Flower
    GO! die #55008 Feathers
    GO! die #55029 Hearts 2"-3"-4"
    GO! die #55017 Strip Cutter $2\frac{1}{2}$" (2" finished)

PREPARATION FOR BLOCKS:
Die cut all pieces as listed below.

Color	#55000 Square $6\frac{1}{2}$"
Black	12 squares
Black print	12 squares

PREPARATION FOR APPLIQUES:
Press fusible web onto the back of all applique
    pieces before cutting.

Die cut all pieces as listed below.

Color	#55012 Circles
Tan	twenty-four 5", four 2"
Green	one 2", two 3"
Blue	two 2", one 3"
Red	one 2", one 3"
Brown	one 3"

Color	#55028 Stars
Green	one 2", one 4"
Blue	four 2", one 4"
Red	one 4"

Color	#55007 Round Flower
Green	seven 1" circles
Blue	three 1" circles, 2 Inside Flowers
Red	3 Flowers, two 1" circles
	4 Inside Flowers

Color	#55029 Hearts
Brown	one 4"
Red	three 2", two 3", three 4"

Color	#55021 Square $2\frac{1}{2}$"
Brown	1 square
Green	1 square

Color	#55008 Feathers
Green	10 feathers
Red	5 teardrops

BASIC APPLIQUE INSTRUCTIONS

1. Fuse lightweight iron-on interfacing on the back of each 6½" square.

2. Iron and then Applique a 5" circle (with Fusible web adhered on the back)

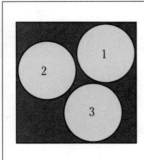

CUTTING TIP
You can cut three 5" circles from each 10" square by being careful in placement.
1. Cut the first circle close to a corner.
2. Cut the second circle between the first circle and close to a corner.
3. Cut the third circle in the remaining space.

3. Iron and then Applique a 4" Heart (with Fusible web adhered on the back)

4. Iron and then Applique a 2" Heart (with Fusible web adhered on the back)

PREPARATION FOR BORDERS & BINDINGS:
Die cut $2\frac{1}{2}$" wide strips x width of fabric (usually 42" - 44").

Color	#55017 Strip Cutter
Black	8 (4 for borders, 4 for binding)

Press lightweight iron-on interfacing onto the back of Black fabric before cutting the squares.

Color	#55021 Square $2\frac{1}{2}$"
Black	4 squares for Cornerstones

-

ASSEMBLY:
Arrange all pieces on a work surface or table.
Applique each square as desired.
Sew the blocks together, 6 rows of 4 blocks per row. Press.
Sew the rows together. Press.
Optional: Applique a 2" Tan square to each cornerstone.

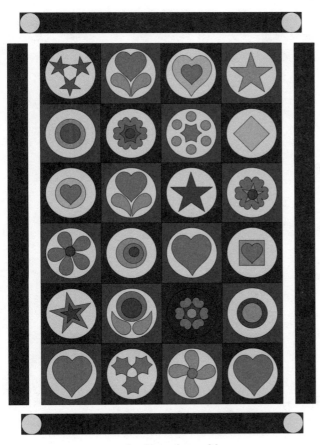

Applique Assembly

Borders:
Cut 2 strips $36\frac{1}{2}$" long for sides.
Cut 2 strips $24\frac{1}{2}$" long for top and bottom.
Sew side borders to the quilt. Press.
Sew a Cornerstone to each end of the top and bottom borders. Press.
Sew top and bottom borders to the quilt. Press.

FINISHING:
Quilting: See Basic Instructions.
Binding: Sew 4 strips together end to end to equal 146".
See Binding Instructions on this page.

Basic Mitered Binding

A Perfect Finish:
The binding endures the most stress on a quilt and is usually the first thing to wear out. For this reason, we recommend using a double fold binding.
1. Trim the backing and batting even with the quilt edge.
2. If possible cut strips on the crosswise grain because a little bias in the binding is a Good thing. This is the only place in the quilt where bias is helpful, for it allows the binding to give as it is turned to the back and sewn in place.
3. Strips are usually cut $2\frac{1}{2}$" wide, but check the instructions for your project before cutting.
4. Sew strips end to end to make a long strip sufficient to go all around the quilt plus 4"- 6".
5. With wrong sides together, fold the strip in half lengthwise. Press.
6. Stretch out your hand and place your little finger at the corner of the quilt top. Place the binding where your thumb touches the edge of the quilt. Aligning the edge of the quilt with the raw edges of the binding, pin the binding in place along the first side.
7. Leaving a 2" tail for later use, begin sewing the binding to the quilt with a $\frac{1}{4}$" seam.

For Mitered Corners:
1. Stop $\frac{1}{4}$" from the first corner. Leave the needle in the quilt and turn it 90°. Hit the reverse button on your machine and back off the quilt leaving the threads connected.
2. Fold the binding perpendicular to the side you sewed, making a 45° angle. Carefully maintaining the first fold, bring the binding back along the edge to be sewn.
3. Carefully align the edges of the binding with the quilt edge and sew as you did the first side. Repeat this process until you reach the tail left at the beginning. Fold the tail out of the way and sew until you are $\frac{1}{4}$" from the beginning stitches.
4. Remove the quilt from the machine. Fold the quilt out of the way and match the binding tails together. Carefully sew the binding tails with a $\frac{1}{4}$" seam. You can do this by hand if you prefer.

Finishing the Binding:
5. Trim the seam to reduce bulk.
6. Finish stitching the binding to the quilt across the join you just sewed.
7. Turn the binding to the back of the quilt. To reduce bulk at the corners, fold the miter in the opposite direction from which it was folded on the front.
8. Hand-sew a Blind stitch on the back of the quilt to secure the binding in place.

Align the raw edge of the binding with the raw edge of the quilt top. Start about 8" from the corner and go along the first side with a $\frac{1}{4}$" seam.

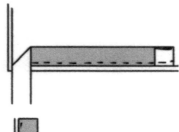

Stop $\frac{1}{4}$" from the edge. Then stitch a slant to the corner (through both layers of binding)... lift up, then down, as you line up the edge. Fold the binding back.

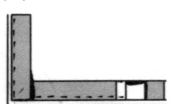

Align the raw edge again. Continue stitching the next side with a $\frac{1}{4}$" seam as you sew the binding in place.

Expanding Borders Quilt

photo is on page 51
SIZE: 64" x 93"
YARDAGE:
We used *Moda* "Marble Swirls".
    $5\frac{1}{2}$ yards White (for blocks, border, & binding)
    $1\frac{1}{3}$ yards Aqua
    $\frac{5}{8}$ yard Blue
    $\frac{3}{4}$ yard Light Green
    $\frac{1}{3}$ yard Dark Green
    1 yard Yellow
    $\frac{3}{4}$ yard Orange
    1 yard Red
    $\frac{1}{3}$ yard Burgundy

Backing   Purchase $5\frac{3}{8}$ yards
Batting   Purchase 72" x 101"
Sewing machine, needle, thread
4 yards of lightweight iron-on interfacing
3 yards of Fusible web

Row of the week or month... this quilt is fun to assemble. You can set a goal to assemble it a little at a time. At the end of months or a year, you'll have a fabulous quilt finished.

ROW OF THE MONTH ASSEMBLY:
TIP: These sections may be assembled in any order. Our suggestion is to begin with the simplest sections, then work up to the diagonal and applique sections.
TIP: When working with odd angles, the length of the piece may vary. If your piece comes up short, simply cut an extra piece and sew it to the end.
Trim all rows to $48\frac{1}{2}$" long.

AccuQuilt® GO!™ Fabric Cutter (#55100),
    (refer to pages 12-13 for dies)
GO! die #55017 Strip Cutter $2\frac{1}{2}$" (2" finished)
GO! die #55001 Triangle $6\frac{1}{2}$"
GO! die #55009 Triangle $3\frac{1}{2}$"
GO! die #55002 Triangle $4\frac{7}{8}$"
GO! die #55016 Triangle Isosceles 5" x 6"
GO! die #55000 Square $6\frac{1}{2}$" (6" finished)
GO! die #55006 Square $3\frac{1}{2}$" (3" finished)

GO! die #55004 Parallelogram $3\frac{3}{4}$" x $3\frac{1}{2}$"
GO! die #55005 Rectangle $3\frac{1}{2}$" x $6\frac{1}{2}$"
GO! die #55020 Tumbler $6\frac{1}{2}$"
GO! die #55007 Round Flower
GO! die #55029 Heart 3"
GO! die #55028 Star 4"

$3\frac{1}{2}$"W x $6\frac{1}{2}$"H Rectangle

Section 13

Section 13:
    Use GO! die #55006 Rectangle $3\frac{1}{2}$" x $6\frac{1}{2}$".
    Cut 4 Light Green and 4 Dark Green rectangles.
    Sew the pieces together Light-Dark etc. to make a section $3\frac{1}{2}$" wide. Press.

$6\frac{1}{2}$" Square

Section 14

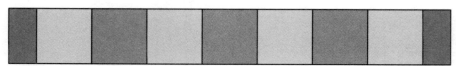

Section 14:
    Use GO! die #55000 Square $6\frac{1}{2}$".
    Cut 5 Aqua and 4 Yellow squares.
    Sew the squares together Aqua-Yellow etc. to make a section $6\frac{1}{2}$" wide. Press.
    Optional Applique:
    die #55029 and die #55028.
    Cut out 4 Orange 3" hearts and 3 White 4" stars. Applique as desired.

$3\frac{1}{2}$" Square

Section 19

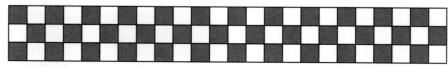

Section 19:
    Use GO! die #Die 55006 Square $3\frac{1}{2}$".
    Cut 16 White and 16 Yellow squares.
    Sew the pieces together to make a checkerboard section $6\frac{1}{2}$" wide. Press.

$2\frac{1}{2}$" Square

OR

Section 3

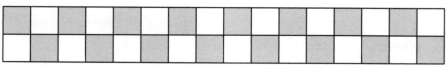

Section 3 - Technique 1:
    Use GO! die #55021 Square $2\frac{1}{2}$".
    Cut 36 Red and 36 White $2\frac{1}{2}$" squares.
    Sew the pieces together to make a checkerboard section $6\frac{1}{2}$" wide. Press.

fold fabric on one end
to cut $2\frac{1}{2}$" x 44" Strips

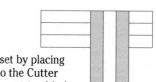

Cross-cut each strip set by placing the strip set back into the Cutter perpendicular to the cutting blades.

OR Section 3 - Technique 2:
    Use GO! die #55017 Strip Cutter $2\frac{1}{2}$".
    Cut 3 Red and 3 White $2\frac{1}{2}$" x 40" strips.
    Sew strips together R-W-R to make a piece $6\frac{1}{2}$" x 30". Press.
    Sew strips together W-R-W to make a piece $6\frac{1}{2}$" x 30". Press.
    Using the Strip Cutter again, cross-cut each strip set by placing the strip set back into the Cutter perpendicular to the cutting blades. Cut into 12 sections $2\frac{1}{2}$" x $6\frac{1}{2}$". Press.
    Sew strips together to make a checkerboard section $6\frac{1}{2}$" wide. Press.

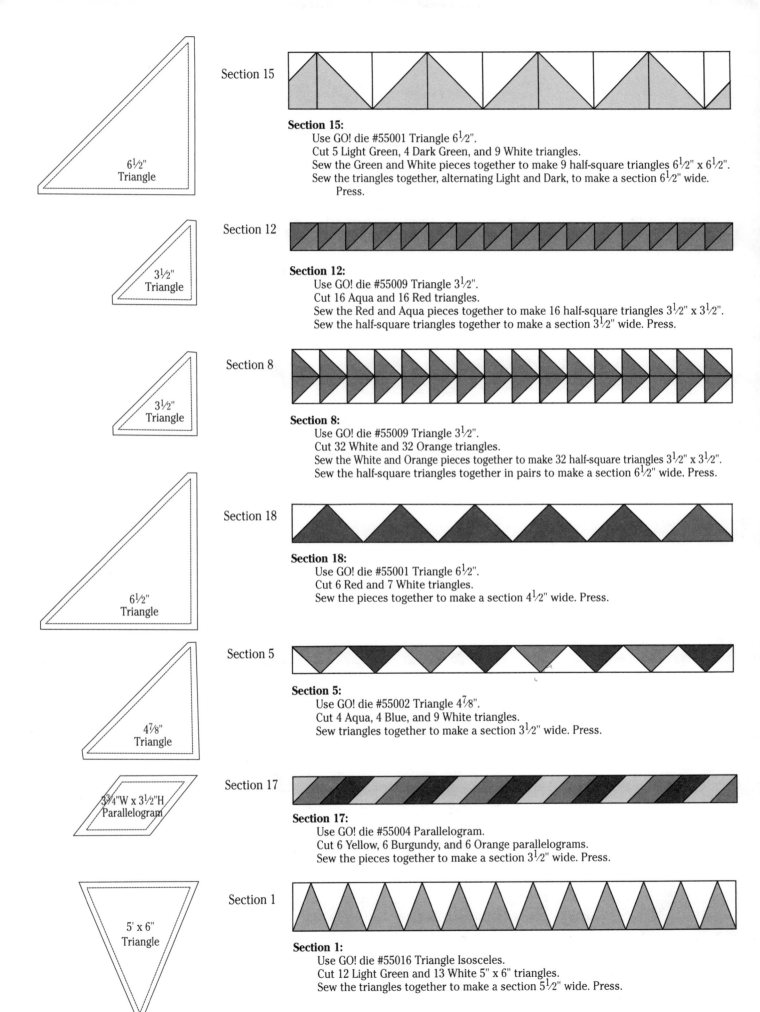

Section 15:
>   Use GO! die #55001 Triangle 6$\frac{1}{2}$".
>   Cut 5 Light Green, 4 Dark Green, and 9 White triangles.
>   Sew the Green and White pieces together to make 9 half-square triangles 6$\frac{1}{2}$" x 6$\frac{1}{2}$".
>   Sew the triangles together, alternating Light and Dark, to make a section 6$\frac{1}{2}$" wide.
>   Press.

Section 12:
>   Use GO! die #55009 Triangle 3$\frac{1}{2}$".
>   Cut 16 Aqua and 16 Red triangles.
>   Sew the Red and Aqua pieces together to make 16 half-square triangles 3$\frac{1}{2}$" x 3$\frac{1}{2}$".
>   Sew the half-square triangles together to make a section 3$\frac{1}{2}$" wide. Press.

Section 8:
>   Use GO! die #55009 Triangle 3$\frac{1}{2}$".
>   Cut 32 White and 32 Orange triangles.
>   Sew the White and Orange pieces together to make 32 half-square triangles 3$\frac{1}{2}$" x 3$\frac{1}{2}$".
>   Sew the half-square triangles together in pairs to make a section 6$\frac{1}{2}$" wide. Press.

Section 18:
>   Use GO! die #55001 Triangle 6$\frac{1}{2}$".
>   Cut 6 Red and 7 White triangles.
>   Sew the pieces together to make a section 4$\frac{1}{2}$" wide. Press.

Section 5:
>   Use GO! die #55002 Triangle 4$\frac{7}{8}$".
>   Cut 4 Aqua, 4 Blue, and 9 White triangles.
>   Sew triangles together to make a section 3$\frac{1}{2}$" wide. Press.

Section 17:
>   Use GO! die #55004 Parallelogram.
>   Cut 6 Yellow, 6 Burgundy, and 6 Orange parallelograms.
>   Sew the pieces together to make a section 3$\frac{1}{2}$" wide. Press.

Section 1:
>   Use GO! die #55016 Triangle Isosceles.
>   Cut 12 Light Green and 13 White 5" x 6" triangles.
>   Sew the triangles together to make a section 5$\frac{1}{2}$" wide. Press.

Expanding Borders Quilt

continued from page 20

Section 10

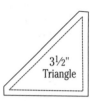

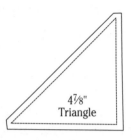

4⅞" Triangle

3½" Triangle

Section 10:
Use GO! die #55002 Triangle 4⅞" and die #55009 Triangle 3½".
Cut 12 large 4⅞" Blue triangles.
Cut 12 small 3½" Yellow and 12 White small 3½" triangles.
Matching the short side of the 3½" triangles, sew Yellow and White triangles together. Press.
Matching each Yellow-White triangle with a Blue, sew the triangles together along
    the long side to make 12 squares, each 4½" x 4½".
Sew the squares together to make a section 4½" wide. Press.

Section 7

6½" Tumbler

Section 7:
Use GO! die #55020 Tumbler 6½".
Cut 6 White, 2 Aqua and 3 Red tumbler shapes .
Sew the pieces together to make a section 6½" wide. Press.

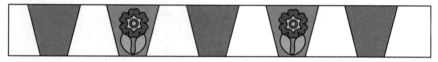

Optional - Applique for Section 7:
Use GO! die #55007 Round Flower.
Press lightweight iron-on interfacing on the back of section 7 to keep it flat.
Press fusible web onto the back of all pieces before cutting.
Cut the following pieces for sections 6 and 7:

22 Light Green leaves	6 Dark Green stems
11 Burgundy flowers	11 Yellow inside flowers
11 Blue 1" circles	11 Orange ⅝" circles

Applique Section 7 as desired. Press.

fold fabric on one end
to cut 2½" x 44" Strips

Section 6

Section 6:
Use GO die #55017 Strip Cutter 2½".
Cut 5 White strips and sew them together end to end. Press.
Cut 4 White strips, each 2½" x 48½" long.
Sew them together side by side to make a section 8½" x 48½".

Optional - Applique for Sections 6:
Line up the position of the flowers over the pots in sections 7. Applique as desired.

Flower

Inside Flower

1" Circle

⅝" Circle

Leaf

Stem

Sew sections 6 and 7 together.

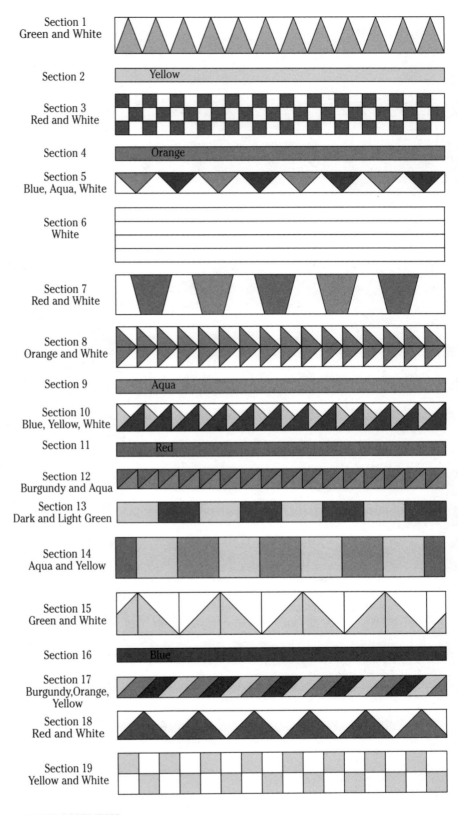

Section 1
Green and White

Section 2
Yellow

Section 3
Red and White

Section 4
Orange

Section 5
Blue, Aqua, White

Section 6
White

Section 7
Red and White

Section 8
Orange and White

Section 9
Aqua

Section 10
Blue, Yellow, White

Section 11
Red

Section 12
Burgundy and Aqua

Section 13
Dark and Light Green

Section 14
Aqua and Yellow

Section 15
Green and White

Section 16
Blue

Section 17
Burgundy, Orange, Yellow

Section 18
Red and White

Section 19
Yellow and White

QUILT ASSEMBLY:

Horizontal Sashing Strips:

Use GO die #55017 Strip Cutter $2\frac{1}{2}$".

Cut the following strips, each $2\frac{1}{2}$" wide 48" long:

4 Aqua (save 2 for the top and bottom borders)

2 Yellow   2 Orange   2 Red   2 Blue

Sew strips together end to end. Cut long strips to $2\frac{1}{2}$" x $48\frac{1}{2}$" to make:

3 Aqua   1 Yellow   1 Orange   1 Red   1 Blue

Arrange all sections and rows on a work surface.
Sew the sections and rows together. Press.

Expanding Borders Quilt

continued from page 20

AQUA BORDERS:

Note:

Before cutting any borders (Aqua or White), measure and check the dimensions.

Sometimes when you sew a lot of seams as in these pieced borders, each seam can expand or contract just a bit to change the size.

This will cause the quilt to grow or shrink so you may need to adjust the length of each border strip.

Border #1:

Sew four $2\frac{1}{2}$" wide Aqua border strips end to end.
Use 2 strips $48\frac{1}{2}$" long for the top and bottom.
Sew the top and bottom borders to the quilt.
Cut 2 strips $81\frac{1}{2}$" long for the sides.
Sew the side borders to the quilt.

Make 4
cornerstone
blocks

WHITE BORDERS:

Border #1:

Border #2:

Sew twenty $2\frac{1}{2}$" wide White border strips end to end.
Cut 6 strips $81\frac{1}{2}$" long for sides.
Cut 6 strips $52\frac{1}{2}$" long for top and bottom.
Sew three $81\frac{1}{2}$" strips together side by side to make a side border $6\frac{1}{2}$" x $81\frac{1}{2}$".
Press. Make 2.
Sew side borders to the quilt. Press.
Sew three $52\frac{1}{2}$" strips together side by side to make a piece $6\frac{1}{2}$" x $52\frac{1}{2}$".
Press. Make 2.

Cornerstones:

Cut 20 Red $2\frac{1}{2}$" squares. Cut 16 White $2\frac{1}{2}$" squares.
Rows 1 & 3: Sew R-W-R. Press.
Row 2: Sew W-R-W. Press.
Sew the rows together. Press. Make 4 cornerstone blocks, each $6\frac{1}{2}$" x $6\frac{1}{2}$".
Sew a cornerstone to each end of the $52\frac{1}{2}$" pieces. Press.
Sew the top and bottom borders to the quilt. Press.

FINISHING:

Quilting: See Basic Instructions.
Binding: Sew 8 strips together end to end to equal 324".
See Binding Instructions on page 19.

Black and White Tote

photo is on page 50
SIZE: 14" x 20½"
YARDAGE:
We used *Moda* "Authentic" by Sweetwater
¾ yard assorted Black prints
½ yard assorted Ivory prints
1½ yards Red print for lining
Batting   Purchase 24" x 44"
Sewing machine, needle, thread
Advantus idea-ology Trinket Pin
AccuQuilt® GO!™ Fabric Cutter (#55100),
      (refer to pages 12-13 for dies)
   GO! die #55017 Strip Cutter 2½" (2" finished)
PREPARATION FOR STRIPS:
Die cut 2½" wide strips x width of fabric (usually 42" - 44").

Color	#55017 Strip Cutter
Assorted Black	9 (4 for tote, 4 for handles, 1 for binding)
Assorted Ivory	3 for tote
Batting	cut 2 strips, each 28½" long

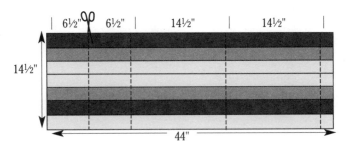

ASSEMBLY:
Sides of Tote:
   Sew 4 Black and 3 Ivory strips together to make a
      piece 14½" x 44". Press.
   Cross cut 2 sections 6½" x 14½" and 2 sections 14½" x 14½".

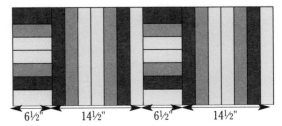

Sides of Tote Assembly:
   Arrange the sections as shown.
   Sew sections together to make a side piece 14½" x 40½".

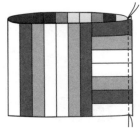 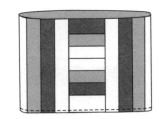

Assemble and Quilt the Tote:
   Cut 1 piece of 14½" x 20¼" lining. Cut 1 piece of 14½" x 20¼" batting.
   Stack a layer of lining, a layer of batting and the panel of the tote.
   Topstitch through all 3 layers to randomly quilt the panel.
Tube Sides of Tote:
   Fold the piece in half (14½" x 20¼"), with right sides together.
   Sew a seam along the 14½" side to form a tube.
Bottom of Tote:
   Rotate the tube, centering the 6½" horizontal strip section.
   Sew a seam along the bottom of the tote.
   Turn the tote right side out.

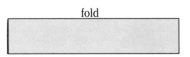

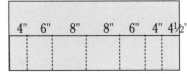

Handles:
   Cut 4 Black strips, each 28½" long.
   Place 2 strips right sides together, with 1 strip of batting on top.
   Sew both long sides to make a tube.
   Turn right sides out. Press. Repeat for the second handle. Set aside.

Cut 2 sections, each 16½" x 40½".   Fold one section in half lengthwise.

4"	6"	8"	8"	6"	4"	4½"

Lay the folded section on top of the flat section.
Topstitch through the layers to form pockets.

Lining:
Cut 2 Red pieces, each 16½" x 40½".
   Fold 1 piece in half to make a pocket section 8¼" x 40½". Press.
   Lay the pocket section on the Red lining, aligning the raw edges.
   Topstitch pocket seams as shown in the diagram.
Fold the piece in half (16½" x 20¼"), with right sides together.
   Sew a seam along the 16½" side to form a tube. Sew along the bottom.

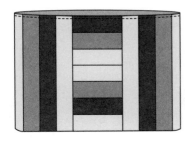 

Extend
handles
1"
above
the top
edge

Assemble the Tote:
   Place the lining into the tote.
   Topstitch ⅛" from the edge around the top.
Bind the Top Edge:
   Pin handles in place (extend 1" above top edge) on the outside of tote.
   Fold the 2½" wide binding strip in half lengthwise. Press.
   Line up the raw edges of the binding with the top of the tote.
   Sew a ¼" seam along the raw edge.
   Turn the binding to the inside and hand stitch in place.
Secure the Handles:
   Topstitch several times over the end of each handle through all layers.

Big Bright Tote

photo is on page 50
SIZE: 12" x18"
YARDAGE:
We used *Moda* "Quilt Diva" by Amy Bradley,
    we purchased 1 'Layer Cake' collection
    of 10" x 10" squares or use leftover fabrics

6 squares	OR	$5/8$ yard Green
4 squares	OR	$1/3$ yard Yellow
6 squares	OR	$5/8$ yard Pink
4 squares	OR	$1/3$ yard Purple
3 squares	OR	$1/3$ yard Blue

Lining   Purchase 2 yards of Yellow
Batting   Purchase 30" x 36"
Sewing machine, needle, thread
$1^1/2$" hook and loop tape
AccuQuilt® GO!™ Fabric Cutter (#55100),
    (refer to pages 12-13 for dies)
    GO! die #55000 Square $6^1/2$" (6" finished)
    GO! die #55006 Square $3^1/2$" (3" finished)
    GO! die #55005 Rectangle $3^1/2$" x $6^1/2$" (3" x 6" finished)
    GO! die #55017 Strip Cutter $2^1/2$" (2" finished)

PREPARATION FOR BLOCKS:
Die cut all pieces as listed below (refer to page 12).

Color	**#55000 Square $6^1/2$"**
Green	4
Yellow	4
Pink	4
Color	**#55005 Rectangle $3^1/2$" x $6^1/2$"**
Green	2
Pink	2
Blue	6
Color	**#55006 Square $3^1/2$"**
Blue	2

PREPARATION FOR HANDLES:
Die cut all pieces as listed below (refer to page 12).

Color	**#55017 Strip Cutter $2^1/2$"**
Purple	Cut 12 strips $2^1/2$" x 10"
Batting	Cut 2 strips $2^1/2$" x 30"

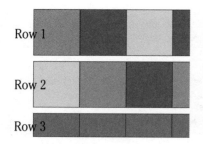

Row 1
Row 2
Row 3

Sew blocks together in rows.
Make 2 of each row.

for side gusset

Sew 3 rows together to make
a purse panel. Make 2.

ASSEMBLY:
Assemble the Side Panels of the Tote:
  Rows 1 & 2:
  Sew 3 squares and a rectangle together to make a piece
    $6^1/2$" x $21^1/2$". Press.
  Row 3:
  Sew 3 rectangles and a square together to make a piece $3^1/2$" x $21^1/2$". Press.
  Sew the rows together for the front panel.
    Press. Repeat for the back panel.

Assemble and Quilt the Tote:
  Cut 2 pieces of 16" x 22" lining. Cut 2 pieces of 16" x 22" batting.
  Stack a layer of lining, a layer of batting and one side panel of the tote.
  Inside each square and rectangle, topstitch through all 3 layers about
    an inch from the seam to quilt the panel.

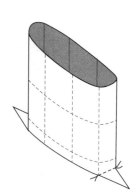

Sew Bottom Gussets:
Stand the tote up and
    fold it into a tube to
    shape a 3" gusset on each
    side, and a 3" flat bottom.
Pull the fabric at the bottom
    of each side gusset into
    a triangle.
Sew across the triangle at the
    bottom of the gusset to
    make a pleat.
Turn the tote right side out.

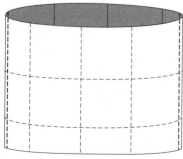

Sew up both sides.

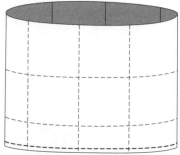

Sew a seam along the bottom.

Sew the Sides of the Tote:
  Position the front side and back side with right sides together.
  Sew the front to the back at the sides to form a tube.

Sew the Bottom of the Tote:
  Rotate the tube, centering the squares in the center of each side panel..

Handles:
  Sew 3 Purple strips end to end to make a piece $2^1/2$" x 29".
    Press. Make 4.
  Place 2 strips right sides together and 1 strip of 2" x 29"
    batting on top.
  Sew both long sides to make a tube.
  Turn right sides out. Press.
  Repeat for the second handle. Set aside.

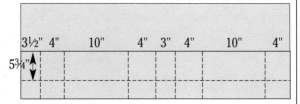

Fold pocket section in half along the top

Lining:

Cut 2 lining pieces, each $15^{1}/2$" x $42^{1}/2$".
Fold 1 piece in half to make a pocket section $7^{3}/4$" x $42^{1}/2$".
Lay the pocket section on top of the large lining, matching the raw edges.
Topstitch pocket seams as in the diagram.

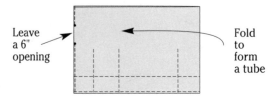

| 3½" | 4" | 10" | 4" | 3" | 4" | 10" | 4" |

5¾"

Make the Pockets

Fold the piece in half ($15^{1}/2$" x $21^{1}/4$"), with right sides together.
Sew a seam along the bottom of the lining.
Topstitch $5^{3}/4$" down from the fold of the pocket.
Leave the lining wrong side out.

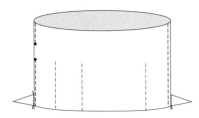

Leave a 6" opening

Fold to form a tube

Sew Pockets into a Tube:

Sew a seam along the $15^{1}/2$" side to form a tube.
Leave a 6" opening near the top for turning.

Sew Bottom Gussets:

As with the tote, stand the lining up.
Form lining into a tube and pull the fabric into a triangle on each side of the bottom.
Sew across the triangle to make a pleat.

Assemble Tote:

Pin the handles in place on the outside of tote.
Place the lining inside of the tote.
Sew a $1/4$" seam around the top edge.
Turn the tote right side out by pulling the quilted side through the opening in the lining.
Push the lining snugly into the tote.
Hand stitch the opening in the lining closed.
Topstitch $1/4$" from the top around the tote.
Topstitch several times over the end of each strap through all layers.

Finish Tote: Sew hook and loop tape to the center top of the inside of the bag as a closure.

Red Hot Purse

photo is on page 50
SIZE: $5^{1}/2$" x $9^{1}/2$"
YARDAGE:
We used *Moda* "Boutique" by Chez Moi
  $1/2$ yard of Red dot
Assorted fabrics for Applique:
  5" x 7" scrap of Green
  8" x 8" scrap of Gold
  2" x 2" scrap of Blue
Sewing machine, needle, thread
39" of Red satin drapery cord for the handle
6" Red zipper
1 yard of Fusible web
2 yards of Lightweight fusible interfacing
AccuQuilt® GO!™ Fabric Cutter (#55100),
  (refer to pages 12-13 for dies)
  GO! die #55017 Strip Cutter $2^{1}/2$" (2" finished)
  GO! die #55007 Round Flower
  GO! die #55029 Hearts - 2", 3", 4"

PREPARATION FOR STRIPS:

Die cut $2^{1}/2$" wide strips x width of fabric
  (usually 42" - 44").

Color	#55017 Strip Cutter
Red	3

PREPARATION FOR APPLIQUES:

Press fusible web onto the back of all pieces before cutting. Die cut pieces as listed below.

Color	**#55007 Round Flower**
Gold	1 Flower
Green	2 Leaves, 1 Stem
Blue	1 Circle 1"
Red	1 Inside Flower

Color	**#55029 Hearts - 3"**
Gold	3 hearts

ASSEMBLY:

Purse Sides:
Cut 3 Red strips, each $2^{1}/2$" x 20".
Sew 3 strips together to make a piece $6^{1}/2$" x 20".
  Press. Cut the piece in half to make 2 sides, each $6^{1}/2$" x 10".

Add Applique Designs:
Applique each side as desired.

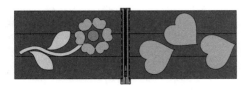

Insert a Zipper:
Lay both purse sides out flat.
Turn the top edges under $1/2$".
Sew a zipper to the top edges.
Open the zipper.

Insert Handles:
Pin handle to each side of the front of purse.
With wrong sides together, sew the sides and bottom of the purse, stitching securely over the handles.
Turn the purse right side out.

Lining:
Cut a Red piece $6^{1}/2$" x 21".
Fold the piece in half with right sides together to make a lining $6^{1}/2$" x $10^{1}/2$".
Sew the sides and bottom of lining.
Press under a top $1/2$" hem.
Slide lining into purse and hand sew lining around the top.

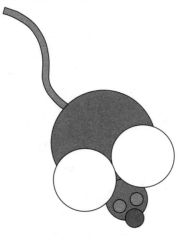

Mouse Assembly
one 1" circle for mouse nose
two ⅝" circles for mouse eyes
1 stem for mouse tail
one 2" circles for mouse head
two 5" circles for mouse body
two 3" circles for mouse ears

Owl Assembly
two 1" circles for owl eyes
three 1" circles for owl nose & toes
2 teardrops for owl ears
two 3" circles for owl eyes
one 5" circle for owl body
two 2" circles for owl eyes

Butterfly Assembly
two 1" circles for butterfly antennae
two 3" circles for butterfly wings
four 2" circles for butterfly wings
two 5" circles for butterfly wings
two 3" circles for butterfly wings
one dragonfly body for butterfly

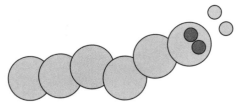

Caterpillar Assembly
two ⅝" circles for caterpillar antennae
two ⅝" circles for caterpillar eyes
six 2" circles for caterpillar body

'Circle Critters'

photo is on page 8
SIZE: approximately 5" to 6" each
AccuQuilt® GO!™ Fabric Cutter (#55100),
    (refer to pages 12-13 for dies)
    GO! die #55012 Circles 2"-3"-5"
    GO! die #55007 Round Flower (use the circles)
    GO! die #55008 Feathers (use the teardrops)
    GO! die #55030 Critters (use the dragonfly body)

PREPARATION FOR APPLIQUES:
Press fusible web onto the back of all pieces before cutting.
Die cut all pieces as listed below.

Color	**#55007 Round Flower**
Green	two 1" circles for bear muzzle
	two 1" circles for bunny muzzle
	two ⅝" circles for caterpillar antennae
Red	three ⅝" circles for bunny eyes, bear nose
	one 1" circle for mouse nose
Blue	seven ⅝" circles for mouse eyes, bunny nose, caterpillar eyes & bear eyes
	eleven 1" circles for ladybug dots, butterfly antennae, owl nose, toes & eyes
	1 stem for mouse tail
Brown	two ⅝" circles for ladybug eyes

Color	**#55008 Feathers**
Red	2 teardrops for owl ears
Cream	2 teardrops for bunny ears
Blue	2 teardrops for bear ears

Color	**#55012 Circles**
Green	ten 2" for bunny feet & caterpillar body
	two 3" for owl eyes
Green	two 3" for butterfly wings (for Quilt)
	two 2" for butterfly wings (for Quilt)
	two 5" for butterfly wings (for Quilt)
Red	two 3" for butterfly wings (for Floorcloth)
	two 2" for butterfly wings (for Floorcloth)
	four 5" for owl body, ladybug wings, & butterfly wings (for Floorcloth)
Blue	one 3" for ladybug head
	four 2" for bear paws
	one 5" for ladybug body
Brown	one 3" for bear head
	one 2" for mouse head
	two 5" for mouse & bear bodies
Cream	five 3" for butterfly wings, mouse ears, bunny head
	four 2" for owl eyes & butterfly wings
	one 5" for bunny body

Color	**#55030 Critters**
Blue	one dragonfly body for butterfly

ASSEMBLY OF CRITTERS:
Lay each critter out on a work surface or table.
Stack circle shapes on the appropriate quilt block or floorcloth backing.
Iron pieces together with fusible web.

Bear Assembly
two 1" circles for bear muzzle
one ⅝" circle for bear nose
two ⅝" circles for bear eyes
2 teardrops for bear ears
four 2" circles for bear paws
one 3" circle for bear head
one 5" circle for bear body

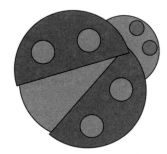

Lady Bug Assembly
four 1" circles for ladybug dots
two ⅝" circles for ladybug eyes
one 5" circle for ladybug wings
one 3" circle for ladybug head
one 5" circle for ladybug body

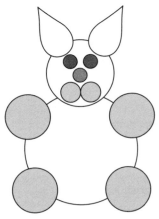

Bunny Assembly
two 1" circles for bunny muzzle
two ⅝" circles for bunny eyes
one ⅝" circle for bunny nose
2 teardrops for bunny ears
four 2" circles for bunny feet
one 3" circle for bunny head
one 5" circle for bunny body

Animal Quilt Assembly Diagram

Toybox Quilt

photo is on page 8
SIZE: 33" x 44$\frac{1}{2}$"

YARDAGE: We used *Moda* "Odyssea" by MoMo,
we also used scraps and leftover fabrics
15" x 15" of Blue for cornerstones and appliques
15" x 15" scrap of Cream
15" x 15" scrap of Green
10" x 14" scrap of Red
10" x 15" scrap of Brown

Blocks & Binding	Purchase 1$\frac{1}{8}$ yards Teal
Border	Purchase $\frac{5}{8}$ yard Brown
Backing	Purchase 1$\frac{1}{2}$ yard
Batting	Purchase 41" x 53"

Sewing machine, needle, thread
4 yards of Fusible web
AccuQuilt® GO!™ Fabric Cutter (#55100),
(refer to pages 12-13 for dies)
GO! die #55017 Strip Cutter 2$\frac{1}{2}$" (2" finished)
GO! die #55021 2$\frac{1}{2}$" Square (2" finished)
GO! dies listed on page 28 for 'circle critters'

PREPARATION FOR BLOCKS:
Cut 6 Teal squares 10" x 10".

PREPARATION FOR SASHING STRIPS:
Die cut all pieces as listed below.

Color	#55017 Strip Cutter
Teal	17 strips 2$\frac{1}{2}$" x 10"

PREPARATION FOR APPLIQUES FOR CRITTERS:
Die cut all pieces as listed on page 28.

PREPARATION FOR BORDERS & BINDINGS:
Die cut 2$\frac{1}{2}$" wide strips x width of fabric (42" - 44").

Color	#55017 Strip Cutter
Brown	8 for borders
Teal	4 for binding

Color	#55021 Squares 2$\frac{1}{2}$" x 2$\frac{1}{2}$"
Blue	12 for cornerstones

ASSEMBLY:
Horizontal sashing strips: Make 4.
Sew Cornerstone-Sashing-
Cornerstone-Sashing-Cornerstone.
Press.
Block Rows: Make 3.
Sew Sash-Square-Sash-Square-Sash.
Press.
Appliques:
Arrange all pieces on a work
surface or table.
Applique as desired.
Sew the rows together. Press.
Border:
Cut 4 strips 37" long for sides.
Sew 2 strips to each side of the
quilt. Press.
Cut 4 strips 33$\frac{1}{2}$" long for top
and bottom.
Sew 2 strips to top and bottom of
the quilt. Press.
FINISHING:
Quilting:
See Basic Instructions.
Binding:
Sew 4 strips together end to end
to equal 165".
See Binding Instructions on page 19.

Rug Assembly Diagram

Decorated Flower Pots

photo is on page 8
SIZE: 8" tall Terra Cotta pot and 6" tall Terra Cotta pot
YARDAGE: Use leftover fabrics in assorted Greens, Blues, Reds, White and assorted prints
Foam brush, *Plaid* Mod Podge
AccuQuilt® GO!™ Fabric Cutter (#55100), (refer to pages 12-13 for dies)
Assorted GO! dies
PREPARATION FOR APPLIQUES: Die cut assorted pieces.
ASSEMBLY: Adhere pieces to pot with *Mod Podge* following the manufacturer's instructions. Coat entire outside of pot with Mod Podge. Let dry.

No Sew Floor Cloth

photo is on page 8
SIZE: 33" x 42"
YARDAGE:
YARDAGE: We used *Moda* "Odyssea" by MoMo,
we also used scraps and leftover fabrics
15" x 20" scrap of Red
15" x 15" scrap of Cream
10" x 15" scrap of Blue
10" x 15" scrap of Brown
10" x 10" scrap of Green

Artist Canvas	Purchase 33" x 42"
Background	Purchase 1 yard Teal
Border	Purchase $\frac{5}{8}$ yard print

Sharpie Black permanent marker
Plaid Mod Podge
AccuQuilt® GO!™ Fabric Cutter (#55100),
(refer to pages 12-13 for dies)
GO! dies listed on page 28 for 'circle critters'
PREPARATION FOR APPLIQUES FOR CRITTERS:
Die cut all pieces as listed on page 28.
ASSEMBLY:
Cut a background fabric 30" x 36".
Adhere background to canvas with Mod Podge.
Cut 4 wavy border strips, each 5" x 42".
Adhere borders around the center, overlapping
the ends and trimming as needed.
Arrange all pieces on mat and adhere in place.
Use a *Sharpie* Black permanent pen to
'pen-stitch' around the shapes as desired.
Apply two coats of Mod Podge as a sealer. Let dry.

Star Pillow Assembly with Prairie Points

Lone Star Pillow

photo is on page 48
SIZE: 12" x 12"
YARDAGE:
We used *Moda* "Blessings" by Brannock & Patek fabrics
        or use leftover fabrics
    15" x 15" scrap of Tan
    7" x 11" scrap of Black solid
    12" x 12" scrap of Burgundy
    15" x 15" scrap of Black print
Backing   Purchase $^1/_4$ yard
Sewing machine, needle, thread
Poly-fil stuffing or 12" pillow form
$^1/_4$ yard of Fusible web
AccuQuilt® GO!™ Fabric Cutter (#55100),
    (refer to pages 12-13 for dies)
    GO! die #55019 Square $4^3/_4$" (4" finished)
    GO! die #55022 Square $2^1/_2$" (2" finished)
    GO! die #55006 Square $3^1/_2$" (3" finished)
    GO! die #55029 Star 4"
    GO! die #55009 Triangle $3^1/_2$" (3" finished)
    GO! die #55017 Strip Cutter $2^1/_2$" (2" finished)

PREPARATION FOR BLOCKS:
Die cut all pieces as listed below.

Color	#55006 Square $3^1/_2$"	#55019 Square $4^3/_4$"
Tan	8 for Prairie Points	1 for Center
Black print	12 for Prairie Points	

Color	#55009 Triangle $3^1/_2$"
Burgundy	4 triangles

Color	#55022 Square $2^1/_2$"
Burgundy	4 squares

Color	#55017 Strip Cutter
Black solid	4 strips $2^1/_2$" x $6^1/_2$"

PREPARATION FOR APPLIQUE STAR:
Press fusible web onto the back of the piece for the star
    before cutting.
Die cut the star.

Color	#55029 Star 4"
Blue	one 4" star

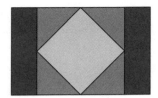

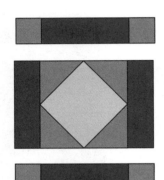

ASSEMBLY:
Assemble the Center Diamond:
    Arrange all pieces on a work surface or table.
    Sew triangles to the Tan square. Press.
    Sew Black border strips to the left and right sides. Press.

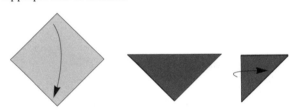

Assemble the Center Block:
    Sew a Burgundy square to 2 Black border strips. Press.
    Sew border strips to top and bottom. Press.

Applique the Star:
    Applique star as desired.

Prairie Points:
1. Fold a $3^1/_2$" square in half.
2. Fold fabric again to form a triangle. Press.

Add Prairie Points:
    Fold Prairie Points and sew to top and bottom as shown. Press.
    Sew Prairie Points to sides, facing inward, with a $^1/_8$" seam. Press.
    Press all Prairie Points to the center of block.

Add Backing to Pillow and Stuff
    Cut 2 backing pieces, each $7^1/_2$" x $12^1/_2$".
    Press under a hem on one $12^1/_2$" side of each backing piece.
    With right sides together, position overlapping backing pieces
        on the pillow (overlapping the hemmed edges in the center).
    Sew around all 4 sides.
    Turn pillow right side out. Press. Stuff pillow.

Dance of the Sunflowers

photo on page 9
SIZE: 32" x 40"
YARDAGE:
We used a *Moda* "Morris Workshop" by Barbara Brackman.
  we purchased 1 'Layer Cake' collection
    of 10" x 10" squares or use leftover fabrics
  7 squares   OR $\frac{5}{8}$ yard Dark Blue
  7 squares   OR $\frac{5}{8}$ yard Green
  7 squares   OR $\frac{5}{8}$ yard Cream/Tan
  4 squares   OR $\frac{1}{3}$ yard Brown
  3 squares   OR $\frac{1}{3}$ yard Red/Orange
Border & Binding   Purchase $\frac{2}{3}$ yard Dark Blue
Backing   Purchase $1\frac{1}{4}$ yards
Batting   Purchase 40" x 48"
Sewing machine, needle, thread
2 yards of Fusible web
AccuQuilt® GO!™ Fabric Cutter (#55100),
    (refer to pages 12-13 for dies)
  GO! die #55021 Triangle $2\frac{1}{2}$" (2" finished)
  GO! die #55021 $4\frac{1}{2}$" Square (4" finished)
  GO! die #55021 $2\frac{1}{2}$" Square (2" finished)
  GO! die #55012 Circles 2", 3", 5"
  GO! die #55007 Round Flower
  GO! die #55017 Strip Cutter $2\frac{1}{2}$" (2" finished)

PREPARATION FOR BLOCKS:
Die cut all pieces as listed below.
  Color   #55021 $4\frac{1}{2}$" Square
  Cream/Tan   24
  Blue   24
From Dark Blue border print, cut triangles.
  Color   #55021 $2\frac{1}{2}$" Triangle
  Green   56
  Dark Blue   56

PREPARATION FOR APPLIQUES:
Press fusible web onto the back of all pieces before cutting.
Die cut all pieces as listed below.
  Color   #55007 Round Flower
  Brown   8 stems, 42 leaves
  Color   #55012 Circles 2", 3", 5"
  Red/Orange   5 each of 2", 3", 5"

PREPARATION FOR BORDER & BINDINGS:
  Color   #55021 $2\frac{1}{2}$" Square
  Dark Blue   4
Die cut $2\frac{1}{2}$" wide strips x width of fabric (usually 42" - 44").
  Color   #55017 Strip Cutter
  Dark Blue   8 (4 for borders, 4 for binding)

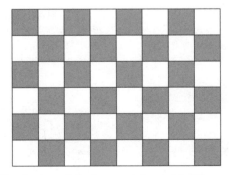

Checkerboard Background Assembly Diagram

ASSEMBLY:
Arrange all pieces on a work surface or table.
Checkerboard:
  Sew the $4\frac{1}{2}$" squares together.
  Make 6 rows of 8 squares per row. Press.
  Sew the rows together. Press.
  Applique as desired.

Sew triangles together along the diagonal to form squares.

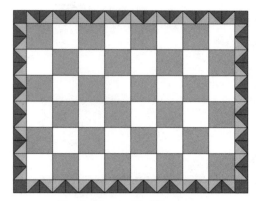

Border Assembly Diagram

Border #1:
  Sew Dark Blue and Green triangles together along the diagonal to form squares.
  Press. Sew squares together to form rectangles. Press.
  Sew rectangles together to form the border rows. Press.
    Sew 2 rows of 6 rectangles for side borders. Press.
    Sew 2 rows of 8 rectangles for top and bottom borders. Press.
  Sew side borders to the quilt. Press.
  Sew a $2\frac{1}{2}$" square to each end of the top and bottom border. Press.
  Sew top and bottom borders to the quilt. Press.

Border #2:
  Cut 2 strips $28\frac{1}{2}$" long for sides.
  Cut 2 strips $40\frac{1}{2}$" long for top and bottom.
  Sew side borders to the quilt. Press.
  Sew top and bottom borders to the quilt. Press.

FINISHING:
Quilting: See Basic Instructions.
Binding: Sew 4 strips together end to end to equal 154".
    See Binding Instructions on page 19.

Dance of the Sunflowers Wall Hanging Assembly Diagram

Make a Basic Pillowcase

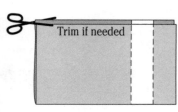

24½" 5¾" 6½"

42½"

Pillowcase Fabric

Border for Opening

Facing for Opening

fold after sewing

1. Sew 3 pieces for each pillowcase.

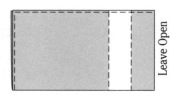

Trim if needed

2. Fold in half, right sides together. Line up edges and cut off any excess.

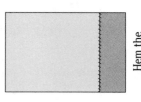

Leave Open

3. Stitch along the edges on 2 sides. Leave 1 side open.

Hem the Opening

4. Fold facing to the inside, fold a hem under and blind stitch the facing in place. Turn pillowcase right side out.

Pillowcases

photo is on page 47
SIZE: 21" x 30" (standard size)
YARDAGE:
We used *Moda* "Boutique" by Chez Moi,
 ⅝ yard Pink/Ivory print
 ¾ yard Pink dot print
 ¾ yard Pink flower print
 ⅓ Red flower print
 ⅙ yard Red dot print
Sewing machine, needle, thread
1 yard of Fusible web
AccuQuilt® GO!™ Fabric Cutter (#55100),
 (refer to pages 12-13 for dies)
 GO! die #55017 Strip Cutter 2½"
 GO! die #55029 Hearts 2", 3" 4"
 GO! die #55009 Triangle 3½"

CUTTING:
Cut the following pieces:
 Pillowcase   25" x 42½"
 Facing for Opening 6½" x 42½"
ASSEMBLY:
Sew a ½" hem on the outer 42½" edge of facing.
Sew pillowcase-border- facing. Press.
Fold pillowcase in half and sew along 2 sides.
Fold back the facing and Blind stitch in place.

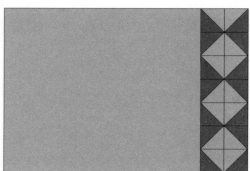

Diamonds Pillowcase Assembly Diagram

1. Make 28 3½" half square triangles.

2. Sew as shown.

3. Sew 6 full diamonds.

4. Make 2 sections like this for ends.

5. Sew 7 blocks together in a long strip

Diamonds Pillowcase

HALF-SQUARE TRIANGLES BORDER:
Die cut 28 Red and 28 Pink triangles.
Sew Red and Pink triangles together to make 28 squares, each 3½" x 3½". Press.
Sew 6 full diamonds and 2 half diamonds as shown to make a piece 6½" x 42½". Press.

Hearts Pillowcase Assembly Diagram

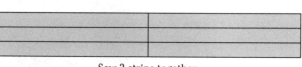

Sew 3 strips together

fold

1. Cut 4 pieces of fabric 5" x 8". Fold to 4" x 5".

fold

2. Lay fabric over heart so that one side of heart overlaps the fold.

3. Die cut and unfold to make connected hearts. Make 4 pairs for a pillowcase.

Heart Pillowcase

PREPARATION FOR APPLIQUES:
Press fusible web onto the back of all pieces before cutting.
Die cut all pieces as listed.
Color #55029 Heart
Red Dot 4 pairs of connected hearts

APPLIQUE BORDER:
Color #55017 Strips
Pink 3 strips x 42½"
Sew the strips together to make a piece 6½" x 42½". Press.
Applique hearts as desired. Press.

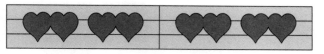

Applique 4 sets of double hearts on the strips

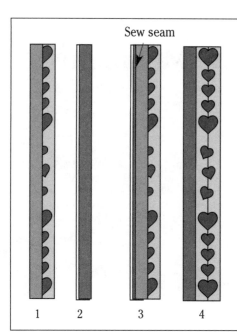

Sew seam

1   2   3   4

ASSEMBLE THE LEFT SIDE:
1. Place a Red strip on top of the appliqued Center stack with right sides together. Align the the raw edges on the left side.
2. Position a Pink strip right side up on top of a batting strip. Place strip and batting under the Center stack, aligning the left edges.
3. Sew a seam $\frac{1}{4}$" from the left edge. Press.

4. Fold the top Pink strip and bottom batting and Pink strips to the left. Press.

Repeat, adding one strip at a time for a total of 1 Red and 6 Pink strips on the left.

ASSEMBLE THE RIGHT SIDE:
Repeat, adding one strip at a time for a total of 6 Pink strips on the right.

'Quilt as You Sew'
'STRIP' TECHNIQUE

This is a simple method that allows you to piece and quilt at the same time.

Add a front strip, batting and a back strip all at one time then turn them to the right side.

Voila, instant quilting with each strip.

Pink Passion Quilt

This 'Quilt as You Sew' technique allows you to make any size quilt, even king size on your home machine. It's a fun way to use up scraps of batting too.

photo is on page 47
SIZE: 32" x 42"

YARDAGE:
We used *Moda* "Boutique" by Chez Moi fabric
    1 yard Pink/Ivory print
    $\frac{3}{4}$ yard Pink dot print
    $\frac{3}{4}$ yard Pink flower print
    $\frac{3}{8}$ Red flower print for appliques & binding
    $\frac{1}{4}$ yard Red dot print

Batting   Purchase 44" x 44"
Sewing machine, needle, thread
1 yard of Fusible web
AccuQuilt® GO!™ Fabric Cutter (#55100),
    (refer to pages 12-13 for dies)
    GO! die #55017 Strip Cutter $2\frac{1}{2}$" (2" finished)
    GO! die #55029 Hearts 2", 3" 4"

PREPARATION FOR STRIPS:
Die cut the following $2\frac{1}{2}$" strips 42" long.

Color	55017 Strip Cutter
Pink/Ivory	11
Pink Dot	9
Pink Flowers	10
Red Dot	2
Batting	14
Red Flowers print	4 for binding

PREPARATION FOR APPLIQUES:
Press fusible web onto the back of pieces before cutting.
Die cut all pieces as listed below.

Color	#55029 Heart
Red prints	nine 2", four 3"

SORTING:
Set aside the following strips for the front of the quilt:
    5 Pink Dot, 4 Pink Flowers, 5 Pink/Ivory, 2 Red Dot.
Label the remaining strips for the back of the quilt.

Batting Front Back   Sandwich

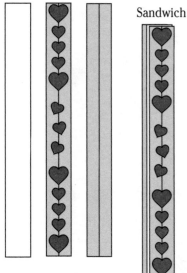

QUILT CENTER :
Cut 1 batting strip $4\frac{1}{2}$" x 42".
Sew 2 Pink strips together to make a piece $4\frac{1}{2}$" x 42". Press.
Sew a second set of 2 Pink strips together for the backing. Press.

APPLIQUE HEARTS:
    Applique hearts to front strip as desired.
    Sandwich the batting between the wrong sides of both Pink strips.
    Pin to prevent shifting.
ASSEMBLE THE LEFT SIDE:
    Place a Red strip on top of the appliqued Center stack with right sides together.
        Align the raw edges on the left side.
    Position a Pink strip right side up on top of a batting strip.
        Place strip and batting under the Center stack, aligning the left edges.
    Sew a seam $\frac{1}{4}$" from the left edge. Press.
        Fold the top Pink strip, and bottom batting and Pink strips to the left. Press.
    Repeat, adding one strip at a time for a total of 1 Red and 6 Pink strips on the left.

ASSEMBLE THE RIGHT SIDE:
    Repeat, adding one strip at a time for a total of 1 Red and 6 Pink strips on the right.
FINISHING:
Binding: Sew 4 strips together end to end to equal 158".
        See Binding Instructions on page 19.

Heart Quilt Assembly Diagram

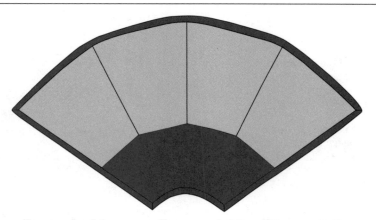

Ranch House Round-Up Place Mats

photo on page 44
SIZE: 11" x 20½"

YARDAGE FOR 4 PLACE MATS:
We used a *Moda* "Happy Camper" by American Jane,
    we purchased 1 'Layer Cake' collection
    of 10" x 10" squares or use leftover fabrics

4 squares	OR	⅓ yard Yellow
4 squares	OR	⅓ yard Red
4 squares	OR	⅓ yard Brown
4 squares	OR	⅓ yard Green

Center curve & Binding   Purchase ⅞ yard Dark Blue
Backing   Purchase ⅝ yard
Batting   Purchase 22" x 42"
Sewing machine, needle, thread
AccuQuilt® GO!™ Fabric Cutter (#55100),
    (refer to pages 12-13 for dies)
    GO! die #55020 Tumbler
    GO! die #55017 Strip Cutter 2½" (2" finished)

PREPARATION FOR BLOCKS:
Cut 4 Dark Blue Center rectangles 7½" x 12½".
Die cut all pieces as listed below (refer to page 12).

Color	#55020 Tumbler
Yellow	4
Red	4
Brown	4
Green	4

PREPARATION FOR BINDING:

Color	#55017 Strip Cutter 2½"
Dark Blue	6 strips 2½" x 42"

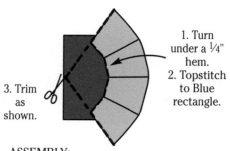

3. Trim as shown.

1. Turn under a ¼" hem.
2. Topstitch to Blue rectangle.

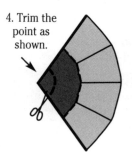

4. Trim the point as shown.

ASSEMBLY:
    Arrange all pieces on a work surface or table.
    For each place mat, sew 4 tumbler shapes together. Press.
    Position the pieced section over the Center rectangle as shown.
    On the pieced section, turn under a ¼" hem.
    Topstitch to Dark Blue rectangle. Press.
    Trim as shown.
    Use place mat as a pattern to cut backing and batting.
FINISHING:
Quilting: See Basic Instructions.
Binding: For each place mat, sew strips together end to end to
    equal 60". See Binding Instructions on page 19.

Summer Cottage in the Mountains

photo is on page 7
SIZE: 52" x 59"

YARDAGE:
We used a *Moda* "Nature's Notebook" by April Cornell,
    we purchased 1 'Layer Cake' collection
    of 10" x 10" squares or use leftover fabrics

22 squares	OR	1¾ yards Light/Yellow
6 squares	OR	⅞ yard Medium Blue
Borders, Binding & Blocks		Purchase 2 yards Medium Blue
Border #2		Purchase ⅔ yard Yellow print
Backing		Purchase 2¾ yards
Batting		Purchase 57" x 67"

Sewing machine, needle, thread
AccuQuilt® GO!™ Fabric Cutter (#55100),
    (refer to pages 12-13 for dies)
    GO! die #55001 Triangle 6½"
    GO! die #55017 Strip Cutter 2½" (2" finished)

PREPARATION FOR SASHING:
Cut 1 Light/Yellow square into 4 strips, each
    2½" x 10" for horizontal sashings.
From all other 10" squares, trim 1 strip
    2½" x 10" for horizontal sashings.

PREPARATION FOR BLOCKS:
Use leftover pieces and Blue yardage to cut the
    following triangles:

Color	#55001 Triangle 6½"
Light/Yellow	42
Blue	42

PREPARATION FOR BORDER & BINDINGS:
Die cut 2½" wide strips x width of fabric (usually 42" - 44").

Color	#55017 Strip Cutter
Dark Blue	18

    (9 for borders, 6 for binding, 3 for sashing)

Yellow print	5

    (for borders #2)

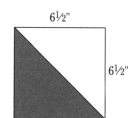
6½"

6½"

Sew Triangles Together
1. Pair 42 Medium Blue triangles with 42
    Light/Yellow triangles. Sew together.

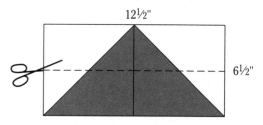
12½"

6½"

Cut Blocks in Half Horizontally
2. Sew Half square triangles together in
    pairs. Cut each set in half horizontally.

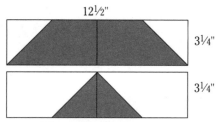

12½"

3¼"

3¼"

Scramble the Parts
3. Arrange all the pieces on the table.
Match them at random.

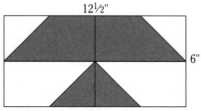

12½"

6"

Sew the Sections Together
4. Sew the sections together to
make new blocks, each 6" x 12½".
Press. Make 21 blocks.

BLOCK ASSEMBLY:

Match each Medium Blue triangle with a Light or Yellow triangle.
Sew the triangles together on the diagonal to make a
6½" x 6½" half-square triangle. Press.
Sew the half-square triangles together in pairs to make 21 pieces
6½" x 12½". Press.
Cut each 6½" x 12½" piece in half to make 42 sections,
each 3¼" x 12½".
Scramble the colors and arrange all pieces on a work surface.
Sew the sections together. Press.

SASHING STRIPS:
Horizontal Sashing Strips:

Randomly sew the Light/Yellow 2½" x 10" sashing strips
end to end. Press.
Cut 18 strips 2½" x 12½".

Vertical Sashing Strips:

Sew 3 Medium Blue 2½" strips end to end. Press.
Cut 2 strips 47½" long.

ASSEMBLY:

Arrange all pieces on a work surface or table.
Assemble 3 columns of 7 blocks each.
Sew a horizontal sashing strip between each block. Press.
Sew the columns together with a vertical sashing strip between
each column. Press.

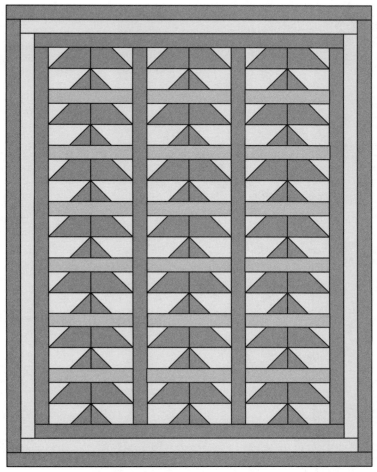

Summer Cottage Quilt Assembly Diagram

BORDERS:
Border #1:
Sew Medium Blue border strips end to end. Press.
Cut 2 strips 50½" long for sides.
Cut 2 strips 44½" long for top and bottom.
Sew side borders to the quilt. Press.
Sew top and bottom borders to the quilt. Press.
Border #2:
Sew Yellow print border strips end to end. Press.
Cut 2 strips 54½" long for sides.
Cut 2 strips 48½" long for top and bottom.
Sew side borders to the quilt. Press.
Sew top and bottom borders to the quilt. Press.
Border #3:
Sew Medium Blue border strips end to end. Press.
Cut 2 strips 58½" long for sides.
Cut 2 strips 52½" long for top and bottom.
Sew side borders to the quilt. Press.
Sew top and bottom borders to the quilt. Press.

FINISHING:
Quilting: See Basic Instructions.
Binding: Sew 4 strips together end to end to equal 239".
See Binding Instructions on page 19.

Front of Quilt Assembly Diagram

Back of Quilt Assembly Diagram

Reversible Cathedral Windows

photo is on page 6

SIZE: 25" x 39"

YARDAGE:

We used a *Moda* "Mill House Inn" by Fig Tree Quilts,
  we purchased 2 'Layer Cake' collections of 10" x 10" squares

20 squares	OR	$1\frac{1}{2}$ yards Lights
20 squares	OR	$1\frac{1}{2}$ yards Darks
2 squares	OR	15" x 15" scrap Red for appliques

Border #1 & Binding	Purchase $\frac{7}{8}$ yard Gold
Batting	Purchase 22" x 45"

Sewing machine, needle, thread

Fusible web

AccuQuilt® GO!™ Fabric Cutter (#55100),
        (refer to pages 12-13 for dies)

  GO! die #55012 Circle 5"
  GO! die #55006 Square $3\frac{1}{2}$" (3" finished)
  GO! die #55028 2" Star
  GO! die #55029 2" Heart
  GO! die #55017 Strip Cutter $2\frac{1}{2}$" (2" finished)

PREPARATION FOR BLOCKS:

Die cut all pieces as listed below (refer to page 12).

Color	#55012 Circle 5"	#55006 Square $3\frac{1}{2}$"
Light colors	60 circles	
Dark colors	60 circles	
Batting		60 squares

PREPARATION FOR BORDERS & BINDINGS:

Die cut $2\frac{1}{2}$" wide strips x width of fabric (usually 42" - 44").

Color	#55017 Strip Cutter
Gold	10 (6 for borders, 4 for binding)

OPTIONAL: PREPARATION FOR APPLIQUES:

Press fusible web onto the back of fabric for hearts and stars before cutting.
Die cut all pieces as listed below (refer to page 13).

Color	#55029 Heart	#55028 Star
Red	eight 2" hearts	eight 2" stars

Applique the pieces to the center of circles as desired.

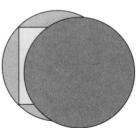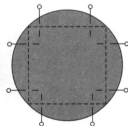

Optional: Applique
a small heart or star in
the center of 16 circles.

Stack two 5" circles
with a $3\frac{1}{2}$" batting
square in the middle.

Pin the layers together
to prevent shifting.

MAKE CIRCLE SANDWICHES:

  Sandwich a batting square between 2 circles, with wrong sides together.
  Pin the layers together to prevent the fabric pieces shifting.
  Repeat for all 60 pairs of circles.

SEW CIRCLES TOGETHER:

  Position 2 circles with the
    backing sides together.
  Topstitch circles together
    along one straight line.
  Continue stitching circles together.

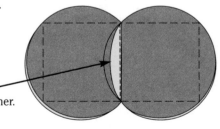

ASSEMBLE CIRCLES INTO ROWS

Topstitch circles together in 10 rows, with 6 circles per row. Press.
  Topstitch rows together in the same method. Press.
    Note: The flaps from the circles will form the Cathedral Windows pattern
        on one side of the quilt, while the back will show the squares.
      Optional: If desired, topstitch or applique stitch the flaps in place.

TRIM THE CENTER:

  Square up and cut the quilt center to $21\frac{1}{2}$" x 36" (measure YOUR quilt to be
  sure this is the correct size to trim off the excess flaps from around the edges).

BORDERS:

  Cut 4 fabric strips and 2 batting strips $35\frac{1}{2}$" long for sides.
  Cut 4 fabric and 4 batting strips $25\frac{1}{2}$" long for top and bottom.
  Note: Measure YOUR quilt to be sure these lengths are correct.

With right sides together, layer border strips and batting:
Each Side: Place 1 fabric strip on the back of the quilt. Place 1
strip and batting on the front, all with the raw edges touching.
Sew a $\frac{1}{4}$" seam along the raw edges. Turn right side out. Press.
Top and Bottom: Repeat as above. Place 1 fabric strip on the
back of the quilt. Place 1 strip and batting on the front, all with
the raw edges touching. Sew a $\frac{1}{4}$" seam along the raw edges.
Turn right side out. Press.

FINISHING:

Binding: Sew 4 strips together end to end to equal 138".
  See Binding Instruction on page 19.

Baby Toys Quilt

photo is on page 46

SIZE: 32" x 38"

YARDAGE:

We used a *Moda* "Boutique" by Chez Moi,
       we purchased 1 'Layer Cake' collection
         of 10" x 10" squares or use leftover fabrics
$\frac{3}{8}$ yard Red
1 yard Gold
16" x 20" scrap of Blue
8" x 12" scrap of Dark Blue
16" x 20" scrap of Light Pink
16" x 16" scrap of Dark Pink
16" x 16" scrap of Green
4" x 6" scrap of White chenille

Backing   Purchase $1\frac{1}{4}$ yards
Batting   Purchase 40" x 46"
Sewing machine, needle, thread
Fusible web
AccuQuilt® GO!™ Fabric Cutter (#55100),
       (refer to pages 12-13 for dies)
       GO! die #55035 Alpha Baby
       GO! die #55037 Baby Baby - duck, bear
       GO! die #55038 Lullaby - rattle, sheep
       GO! die #55000 Square $6\frac{1}{2}$" (6" finished)
       GO! die #55017 Strip Cutter $2\frac{1}{2}$" (2" finished)

PREPARATION FOR BLOCKS:

Die cut all pieces as listed below (refer to page 12).

Color	#55000 Square $6\frac{1}{2}$"
Light Pink	4
Dark Pink	4
Gold	4
Blue	4
Green	4

PREPARATION FOR APPLIQUES:

Press fusible web onto the back of all pieces before cutting.
Die cut all pieces as listed below (refer to page 13).

Color	#55038 Lullaby - rattle, sheep
Dk. Blue sheep parts	2 Legs, 1 Face, 1 Ear
White chenille	1 Sheep body
Lt. Pink	4 Rattle handles
Red	4 Rattle circles
Dk. Blue	4 Rattle stripes

Color	#55037 Baby Baby - duck, bear
Dk. Blue	3 Bear bodies
Gold	2 Duck bodies
Red	2 Duck wings, 2 Duck beaks
	2 sets of Bear ears, paws, bowtie
Lt. Pink	1 set Bear ears, paws, bowtie

Color	#55035 Alpha Baby
Red	Die Cut letters B, A, B, Y

PREPARATION FOR BORDERS & BINDINGS:

Die cut $2\frac{1}{2}$" wide strips x width of fabric (usually 42" - 44").

Color	#55017 Strip Cutter
Red	3 for border #1
Gold	8 (4 for borders, 4 for binding)

LAYOUT AND APPLIQUE:

    Arrange all pieces on a work surface or table.
    Applique designs on blocks as desired.
    Satin stitch eyes and noses with Black thread.

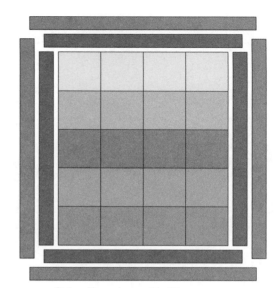

Baby Toys Assembly Diagram

ASSEMBLY:

    Sew blocks together in 5 rows, 4 blocks per row. Press.
    Sew rows together. Press.

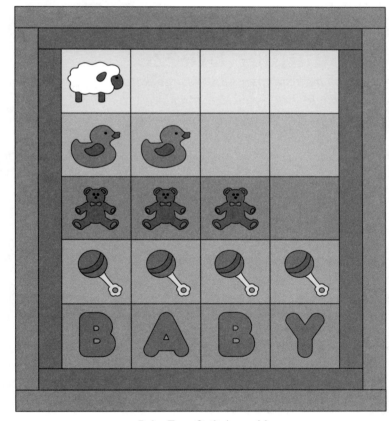

Baby Toys Quilt Assembly

BORDERS:

Red Border #1:
    Cut 2 strips $30\frac{1}{2}$" long for sides.
    Cut 2 strips $28\frac{1}{2}$" long for top and bottom.
    Sew side borders to the quilt. Press.
    Sew top and bottom borders to the quilt. Press.

Gold Border #2:
    Cut 2 strips $34\frac{1}{2}$" long for sides.
    Cut 2 strips $32\frac{1}{2}$" long for top and bottom.
    Sew side borders to the quilt. Press.
    Sew top and bottom borders to the quilt. Press.

FINISHING:

Quilting: See Basic Instructions.
Binding: Sew 4 strips together end to end to equal 150".
    See Binding Instructions on page 19.

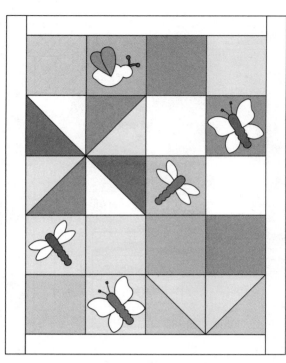

Summer Breeze Quilt Assembly

Summer Breeze

This light summer quilt has no batting. It is easy to stitch vertical rows of quilting right through the chenille backing.

photo is on page 6
SIZE: 28" x 34"
YARDAGE:
We used *Moda* "Old Primrose Inn" by Blackbird Designs, we purchased 1 'Layer Cake' collection of 10" x 10" squares or use leftover fabrics

10 squares	OR	$^7/8$ yard Green
6 squares	OR	$^5/8$ yard Gold/Tan
4 squares	OR	$^1/3$ yard Pink
1 square	OR	5" x 6" scrap of Burgundy

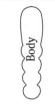

for butterfly and dragonfly

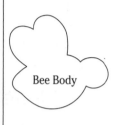

Bee Wings

Bee Body

Bee Antenna

Tips for Applique
Die-cut the body of a butterfly or dragonfly from one color. Diecut bee wings and antennae from a second color. Add this layer to your applique. Satin Stitch or embroider the antennae.

Border #1 & Binding   Purchase $^5/8$ yard Tan
Backing & Appliques   Purchase 1 yard Ivory chenille
Sewing machine, needle, thread
2 yards of Fusible web
AccuQuilt® GO!™ Fabric Cutter (#55100),
(refer to pages 12-13 for dies)
   GO! die #55001 Triangle $6^1/2$" (6" finished)
   GO! die #55000 Square $6^1/2$" (6" finished)
   GO! die #55030 Critters - bee, butterfly, dragonfly
   GO! die #55017 Strip Cutter $2^1/2$" (2" finished)

PREPARATION FOR BLOCKS:
Die cut all pieces as listed below (refer to page 12).

Color	#55001 Triangle	#55000 Square
Gold/Tan	2	5
Green	6	7
Pink	4	2

PREPARATION FOR APPLIQUES:
Press fusible web onto the back of all pieces before cutting.
Die cut all pieces as listed below (refer to page 13).

Color	#55030 Critters
Green	2 Dragonfly bodies, 1 Bee wing
Burgundy	2 Dragonfly bodies, 1 Bee antennae
Chenille	1 Bee, 2 Dragonflies, 2 Butterflies

PREPARATION FOR BORDERS & BINDINGS:
Die cut $2^1/2$" wide strips x width of fabric (usually 42" - 44").

Color	#55017 Strip Cutter
Gold/Tan	8 (4 for borders, 4 for binding)

ASSEMBLY:
Arrange all pieces on a work surface or table.
Sew triangles together along the diagonal to form $6^1/2$" squares.
Applique critters to each block as desired.
Sew blocks together in 5 rows, 4 blocks per row. Press.
Sew rows together. Press.
Border:
Cut 2 strips $24^1/2$" long for top and bottom.
Cut 2 strips $34^1/2$" long for sides.
Sew top and bottom borders to the quilt. Press.
Sew side borders to the quilt. Press.
Quilting
Topstitch with vertical lines 2" apart (go around the critters)
FINISHING:
Quilting: See Basic Instructions.
Binding: Sew 4 strips together end to end to equal 134".
See Binding Instructions on page 19.

Mini Pillows

photo is on page 6
SIZE: Dragonfly: $6^1/2$" x $6^1/2$", Heart: 8" x 8"
YARDAGE:
We used from *Moda* "Old Primrose Inn"
   $8^1/2$" x 12" scrap of Pink
   $6^1/2$" x 10" scrap of Green
   4" x 4" scrap of Burgundy

Binding   Purchase $^1/6$ yard Tan
Backing & Appliques   Purchase $^1/4$ yard White chenille
Sewing machine, needle, thread
Poly-fil stuffing, 1 yard of Fusible web
AccuQuilt® GO!™ Fabric Cutter (#55100),
(refer to pages 12-13 for dies)
   GO! die #55029 Heart 2" & 4"
   GO! die #55030 Critters
   GO! die #55017 Strip Cutter $2^1/2$" (2" finished)

PREPARATION FOR BLOCKS:
Die cut all pieces as listed below (refer to page 12).

Color	#55017 Strip Cutter
Green	3 strips x $6^1/2$"
Pink	4 strips x $8^1/2$"

PREPARATION FOR APPLIQUES:
Press fusible web onto the back of all pieces before cutting.
Die cut all pieces as listed below (refer to page 13).

Color	#55030 Critters
Burgundy	1 Dragonfly body, 2" Heart
Chenille	4" Heart, 1 Dragonfly

PREPARATION FOR BINDINGS:
Die cut $2^1/2$" wide strips x width of fabric (usually 42" - 44").

Color	#55017 Strip Cutter
Tan	2 (1 for each pillow)

Heart Pillow

ASSEMBLY:
Arrange all pieces on a work surface or table.
Sew Pink strips to make an $8^1/2$" x $8^1/2$" square.
Sew Green strips to make a $6^1/2$" x $6^1/2$" square.
Applique critters to blocks as desired.
Cut chenille backings: two $5^1/2$" x $8^1/2$", two 5" x $6^1/2$".
Sew backings to pillows, overlapping in the center.
Sew binding (instructions on page 19.) Stuff pillow.

Dragonfly Pillow

'Quilt as You Sew' 'ROUND' TECHNIQUE

This is a simple method that allows you to piece and quilt at the same time.

  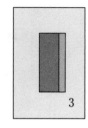  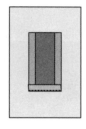 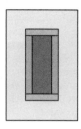

POSITION THE CENTER ROW:
Work on a flat work surface or table.
1. Center a Row (the Center Row with the diamonds for this quilt) over the backing and batting.
Pin the Center Row in place.

ADD ONE BORDER STRIP AT A TIME:
2. Line up a border strip along the raw edge of the Center Row with right sides together. Sew a seam $1/4$" from the raw edge.
3. Turn the strip over next to the Center Row. Press.

ADD MORE STRIPS:
4. Add additional strips in the same manner, working around the Center Row until the quilt is finished.

Scraps of Sunlit Sky

This is a wonderful 'quilt as you go' design that can be completed quickly.

 Rows 1, 3, 5

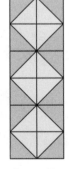 Rows 2, 4, 6

photo is on page 46
SIZE: 26" x 38"
YARDAGE:
We used *Moda* "Nature's Notebook" by April Cornell fabrics
   $1/2$ yard Blue print
   $7/8$ yard Yellow small print for strips & binding
   $1/2$ yard Yellow large print
   3" x 8" scrap of Medium Blue for appliques
Backing   Purchase $1 1/3$ yards
Batting   Purchase 34" x 46"
Sewing machine, needle, thread
Optional - 1 yard of Fusible web
AccuQuilt® GO!™ Fabric Cutter (#55100),
    (refer to pages 12-13 for dies)
    GO! die #55009 Triangle $3 1/8$" (3" finished)
    GO! die #55017 Strip Cutter $2 1/2$" (2" finished)
    GO! die #55029 2" Heart (optional)

PREPARATION FOR BLOCKS:
Die cut all pieces as listed below (refer to page 12).

Color	#55009 Triangle
Blue print	12
Yellow small print	12

PREPARATION FOR BORDERS & BINDINGS:
Die cut $2 1/2$" wide strips x width of fabric (usually 42" - 44").

Color	#55017 Strip Cutter
Yellow large print	5
Yellow small print	7 (3 for borders, 4 for binding)
Blue print	5

OPTIONAL - APPLIQUES:
Press fusible web onto the back of all pieces before cutting.
Die cut all pieces as listed below (refer to page 13).

Color	#55029 2" Heart
Medium Blue	3

ASSEMBLY FOR CENTER:
    Arrange all pieces on a work surface or table.
    Sew triangles together along the diagonal to form squares. Press.
    Sew squares together in 6 rows of 2 squares each. Press.
    Sew the rows together. Press. Applique hearts as desired.

'QUILT AS YOU SEW' TECHNIQUE:
See 'Quilt as You Sew' technique instructions above.
    Work on a flat work surface or table.
    Center the Center Row over the backing and batting.
    Pin the Center Row in place.
    Add the first row of borders by following the
        'Quilt as You Sew' instructions above.
    Add additional rows of borders to complete the top.

Center Row

Add the first 'round' of 'Quilt as You Go' border.

Scraps of Sunlit Sky Quilt Assembly Diagram

BORDERS FOR 'QUILT AS YOU GO':
Blue Print Border #1:
    Cut 2 strips $18 1/2$" long for sides.
    Cut 2 strips $10 1/2$" long for top and bottom.
    Sew side borders to the quilt. Press.
    Sew top and bottom borders to the quilt. Press.
Large Yellow Print Border #2:
    Cut 2 strips $22 1/2$" for sides and 2 strips $14 1/2$" long.
    Sew side borders and top and bottom to quilt. Press.
Small Yellow Print Border #3:
    Cut 2 strips $26 1/2$" for sides and 2 strips $18 1/2$" long.
    Sew side borders and top and bottom to quilt. Press.
Blue print Border #4:
    Cut 2 strips $30 1/2$" for sides and 2 strips $22 1/2$" long.
    Sew side borders and top and bottom to quilt. Press.
Large Yellow Print Border #5:
    Cut 2 strips $34 1/2$" for sides and 2 strips $26 1/2$" long.
    Sew side borders and top and bottom to quilt. Press.
FINISHING:
Quilting: See Basic Instructions.
Binding: Sew 4 strips together end to end to equal 138".
    See Binding Instructions on page 19.

Fall Rhapsody Quilt

photo on page 49
SIZE: 46" x 62"

YARDAGE:
We used a *Moda* "Blessings" by Brannock & Patek,
     we purchased 2 'Layer Cake' collections
     of 10" x 10" squares or use leftover fabrics

17 squares	OR	$1\frac{1}{2}$ yards Brown
17 squares	OR	$1\frac{1}{6}$ yards Tan
13 squares	OR	$1\frac{1}{6}$ yards Blue
10 squares	OR	$\frac{7}{8}$ yard Green
7 squares	OR	$\frac{5}{8}$ yard Red
6 squares	OR	$\frac{5}{8}$ yard Black

     Optional: Use any leftover fabrics for the Prairie Points

Sashing strips & triangles   Purchase 1 yard of Black print
Border & Binding   Purchase 2 yards of Black solid
Backing   Purchase $2\frac{2}{3}$ yards
Batting   Purchase 54" x 70"
Sewing machine, needle, thread
6 yards of Fusible web
Optional: 6 yards of $\frac{1}{4}$" fusible bias tape - *Clover* Quick Bias
AccuQuilt® GO!™ Fabric Cutter (#55100),
     (refer to pages 12-13 for dies)
     GO! die #55002 Triangle $4\frac{7}{8}$"
     GO! die #55021 Triangle $2\frac{1}{2}$" (2" finished)
     GO! die #55006 Square $3\frac{1}{2}$" (3" finished)
     GO! die #55021 Square $2\frac{1}{2}$" (2" finished)
     GO! die #55017 Strip Cutter $2\frac{1}{2}$" (2" finished)
     GO! die #55041 Fall Medley - pumpkin, leaf, acorn, large leaf

PREPARATION FOR BLOCKS:
Die cut all pieces as listed below.

Color	#55002 Triangle $4\frac{7}{8}$"
Tan	24
Blue	8
Black	16

Color	#55021 Triangle $2\frac{1}{2}$"
Tan	96
Blue	48
Black	48

Color	#55021 Square $2\frac{1}{2}$"
Red	3 block centers, 6 sashing cornerstones
Tan	3 block centers, 6 sashing cornerstones
Blue stripe	12 block cornerstones
Red stripe	12 block cornerstones

PREPARATION FOR SASHINGS & BINDING:
Die cut $2\frac{1}{2}$" wide strips x width of fabric (usually 42" - 44").

Color	#55017 Strip Cutter
Black solid	6 strips
Black print	7 strips

Make 24 large squares

Make 96 small squares

BLOCK ASSEMBLY:
Large Squares:
    Pair each Tan $4\frac{7}{8}$" triangle with a Black or Blue triangle. Sew
      triangles together along the diagonal to form 24 large squares. Press.
Small Squares:
    Pair each Tan $2\frac{1}{2}$" triangle with a Black or Blue triangle. Sew
      triangles together along the diagonal to form 96 small squares. Press.

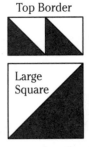

Top Border
Side Border
Large Square

Note the direction of the diagonals.
Make 24 large squares. Make 24 top borders (2 small squares).
Make 24 side borders (2 small squares & 1 corner).

BLOCKS:
    Arrange all $2\frac{1}{2}$" corners, small and large squares on a work surface.
    Note The Blue pieces will form Blocks 1, 4 & 5.
          The Black pieces will form Blocks 2, 3 & 6.

Top Borders:
    Sew 2 small squares together. Press.
    Sew top borders to the top of each $4\frac{1}{2}$" large square. Press.
Side Borders:
    Sew a corner and 2 small squares together. Press.
    Sew side borders to the left hand side of each block. Press.

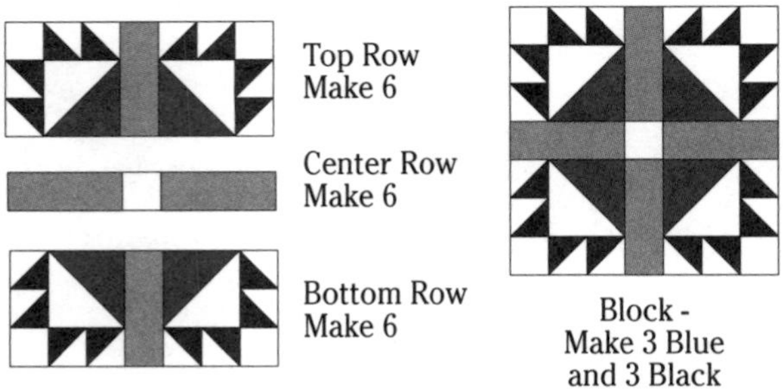

Top Row Make 6
Center Row Make 6
Bottom Row Make 6
Block - Make 3 Blue and 3 Black

Small Sashing Strips:
    Cut 24 Brown sashing strips, each $2\frac{1}{2}$" x $6\frac{1}{2}$".
    Use 3 Red block centers and 3 Tan block centers, each a $2\frac{1}{2}$" square.
Assemble the Rows for the Blocks:
    Top Row: Sew a Block-Sashing strip-Block. Press.
    Center Row: Sew a Sashing strip-Square-Sashing Strip. Press.
    Bottom Row: Sew a Block-Sashing strip-Block. Press.
Assemble the Blocks:
    Top Row: Sew a Block-Sashing strip-Block. Press.

Block Row

BLOCKS:
    Arrange all pieces on a work surface or table.
    Note All block sashing strips are Brown.
          The Blue blocks have Tan centers.
          The Black blocks have Red centers.
Block Rows A and C (make 3):
    Sew a Sashing-Blue Block-Sashing-Black Block-Sashing.
Block Row B: Turn 1 row of blocks upside down so Black is on the left.

Sashing Rows 1 & 3
Sashing Rows 2 & 4

Horizontal Sashing Rows:
Cut 17 Black print $2\frac{1}{2}$" x $14\frac{1}{2}$" sashing strips.
    Rows 1 & 3: Sew a Red square-Black sashing strip-Tan
      square-Black sashing strip-Red square. Press.
    Rows 2 & 4: Sew a Tan square-Black sashing strip-
      Red square-Black sashing strip-Tan square. Press.

Sashing Row 1

Blocks Row A
Blue-Black

Sashing Row 2

Blocks Row B
Black-Blue

Sashing Row 3

Blocks Row C
Blue-Black

Sashing Row 4

Block 1 Blue

Block 2 Black

Block 3 Black

Block 4 Blue

Block 5 Blue

Block 6 Black

QUILT ASSEMBLY:
Arrange all pieces on a work surface or table.
Sew the rows together: Rows 1-A-2-B-3-C-4. Press.

PREPARATION FOR APPLIQUES:
Press fusible web onto the back of all pieces before cutting.
Die cut all pieces as listed below.

Color	#55041 Fall Medley - pumpkin, leaf, acorn, large leaf
Red	4 maple leaves, 10 acorns, 10 pumpkins, 4 leaves
Green	8 maple leaves, 10 acorn tops, 8 oak leaves

Cut and Applique the Borders

Fall Rhapsody before bias tape wavy line and Prairie Points

Applique Border:
Cut strips 6$\frac{1}{2}$" wide parallel to the selvage to eliminate piecing.
Cut 2 strips 50$\frac{1}{2}$" long for sides.
Cut 2 strips 46$\frac{1}{2}$" long for top and bottom.

Applique Pieces on the Border Strips:
Applique as desired (refer to the position of applique pieces).

Sew Border to the Quilt:
Sew side borders to the quilt. Press.
Sew top and bottom borders to the quilt. Press.

Optional: **Add the Wavy Line:**
Topstitch $\frac{1}{4}$" bias tape in a wavy line around the shapes.

Fall Rhapsody Border Assembly - with Prairie Points

FINISHING:
Quilting: See Basic Instructions.

Optional Prairie Points:
GO! die #55006 Square 3$\frac{1}{2}$" for Prairie Points
Die cut 90 from assorted colors
Fold each 3$\frac{1}{2}$" square to make a Prairie Point as shown.
Align Prairie Points along the edge of the quilt.
Pin in position with raw edges together.
Topstitch Prairie Points in place along the edges $\frac{1}{8}$" from the edge.

Prairie Points:
1. Fold a 3$\frac{1}{2}$" square in half.
2. Fold fabric again to form a triangle. Press.

Binding: Sew 6 strips together end to end to equal 226".
Fold and press binding lengthwise.
Position binding on the right side of the quilt with raw edges together.
Stitch along the edge $\frac{1}{4}$" from the edge.
Turn binding about $\frac{3}{4}$" to the back and hand stitch the folded edge.

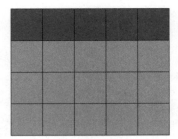

Make the Background
then add Applique pieces

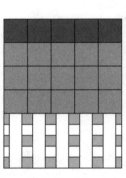

Grass
Make 6

Posts
Cut 5

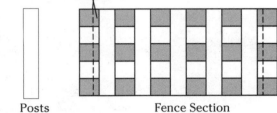

Fence Section
Center and trim to 10" x 20½"

Make the Fence Section

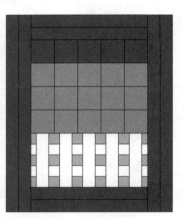

Assemble Background
and Fence Section

Add Borders

Garden Delight Quilt Assembly Diagram

Garden Delight

photo on page 43
SIZE: 28" x 34"

YARDAGE:

We used a *Moda* "Happy Campers" by American Jane,
    we purchased 1 'Layer Cake' collection
      of 10" x 10" squares or use leftover fabrics

4 squares	OR	⅓ yard Medium Blue
4 squares	OR	⅓ yard Green for fence & appliques
2 squares	OR	⅓ yard Dark Blue
2 squares	OR	⅓ yard Cream for fence
2 squares	OR	⅓ yard Gold for appliques
3 squares	OR	⅓ yard Red for appliques
2 squares	OR	⅓ yard Brown for appliques

Border & Binding Purchase ⅞ yard Navy
Backing   Purchase 1 yard
Batting   Purchase 36" x 42"
Sewing machine, needle, thread
3 yards of Fusible web
AccuQuilt® GO!™ Fabric Cutter (#55100),
      (refer to pages 12-13 for dies)
    GO! die #55007 Round Flower
    GO! die #55030 Critters
    GO! die #55012 Circle 5"
    GO! die #55021 Square 2½", 4½" (2" & 4" finished)
    GO! die #55017 Strip Cutter 2½" (2" finished)

PREPARATION FOR BLOCKS:
Die cut all pieces as listed below.

Color	#55021 Square	#55017 Strip Cutter
Med. Blue	15 (4½")	
Navy	5 (4½")	
Cream	12 (2½")	5 strips 2½" x 10"
Green	18 (2½")	

PREPARATION FOR APPLIQUES:
Press fusible web onto the back of all pieces before cutting.
Die cut all pieces as listed below.

Color	#55007 Round Flower - petals, centers, leaf, stem
Brown	9 stems, 5 flower centers
Green	10 leaves
Red	2 flowers, 3 flower insides
Gold	3 flowers, 2 flower insides

Color	#55030 Critters - bee, butterfly, dragonfly
Brown	2 dragonfly bodies
Gold	1 dragonfly
2 different Reds	1 butterfly wing

Color	#55012 Circle 5"
Red	2
Gold	1

PREPARATION FOR BORDERS & BINDINGS:
Die cut 2½" wide strips x width of fabric (usually 42" - 44").

Color	#55017 Strip Cutter
Dark Blue	10 (6 for borders, 4 for binding)

ASSEMBLY:

Background: Arrange all pieces on a work surface or table.
    Sew squares together in 4 rows of 5 squares each. Press.
    Sew the rows together. Press.

Fence Section: Set aside 5 Cream strips for vertical posts.
    Sew squares together G-C-G-C-G for grass. Press. Make 6.
    Sew strips and posts together to make a piece 10" x 22½". Press.
    Trim equally on each side to make a piece 10" x 20½".

Border #1:
    Cut 4 strips 20½" long for top and bottom.
    Sew 2 strips to top and bottom of the quilt. Press.
    Cut 4 strips 34½" long for sides.
    Sew 2 strips to each side of the quilt. Press.

FINISHING:

Quilting: See Basic Instructions.
Binding: Sew 4 strips together end to end to equal 134".
    See Binding Instructions on page 19.

Garden Delight

pieced by Janice Irick

quilted by Sue Needle

Even in the city, tiny flower gardens robustly withstand the encroachments of concrete and noise, providing a natural respite from the rush of the day.

This happy collection of flowers welcomes sunshine and rain, and invites butterflies, dragonflies, and the appreciative eye to share both fragrances and colors. Take a moment to relax and make this pretty wall hanging for your kitchen, sunroom, porch, or patio.

instructions on page 42

Ranch House Round Up

sewn by
Janice Irick

Gather the family 'round the table for a summer feast that is sure to please the eye as well as the palate. Retro fabric prints make these curved place mats a real treat.

They are designed to fit on a circular table.

instructions on page 34

Summer's Buzz

pieced by
Donna Arends Hansen

quilted by
Sue Needle

Make your summer picnic more fun with place mats that flutter with seasonal motifs.

Butterflies and dragonflies flit across the surface of these attractive place settings.

instructions on page 16

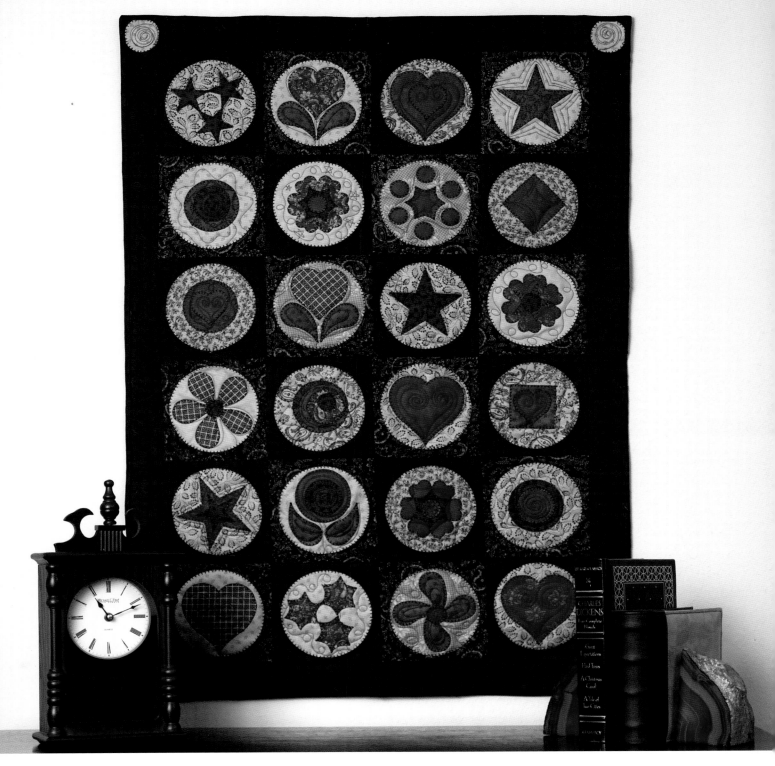

Pennsylvania Dutch

pieced by Donna Arends Hansen

quilted by Sue Needle

For over 300 years, the Pennsylvania Dutch have decorated their homes and documents with the traditional symbols of the Rhineland. The popular six pointed star, or hex, inspired the term commonly used to describe these motifs. Each bright, colorful design has meaning: hearts for love, birds (called distelfinks) for luck and happiness, tulips for faith, and stars for good luck. Blue conveyed protection, white purity, green abundance and red strong emotion.

You can easily create a quilt with special meaning and carry on a time-honored American tradition.

instructions on pages 18 - 19

Scraps of Sunlit Sky

sewn by Betty Nowlin

Brighten any room with these sky blue prints lit by pastel yellows. This natural color combination is as soothing as a summer day and will soften a wall, cheer up your favorite chair, and warm your heart every time you see it.

Sized for a crib, this lovely quilt would be a perfect gift for a baby shower.

instructions on page 39

Baby Toys

pieced by
Betty Nowlin

quilted by
Sue Needle

Wonderful as a wall hanging or a crib blanket, this sweet quilt may be your child's first favorite blankie that goes everywhere.

Charming motifs are so easy to create with the Accu-Cut GO! Easy appliques make this a fabulous beginner quilt or charity project.

instructions on page 37

Passion for Linens

pillows by Donna Arends Hansen, quilt by Donna Perrotta

Beautiful linens dress up a bedroom, creating a welcome feeling for guests, and make the room a fun place to be.

instructions on pages 32 - 33

Placemat and Table Runner Sampler

pieced by Donna Perrotta

quilted by Sue Needle

Do you love sampler blocks but don't have much time? Here's your chance to indulge your passion in a small project.

The solid alternate blocks make this quick and fun to assemble.

Whether you have leftover pieces from making the Place Mats, or you just couldn't stop yourself from making these striking blocks, here's a fun way to use up those extra pieces with an attractive Table Runner.

instructions on page 17

Fall Rhapsody Quilt

pieced by Donna Perrotta

quilted by Sue Needle

Listen to the music of rustling leaves as they tumble into neatly raked piles.

Jack Frost paints the pumpkins with crystal glaze while Nature invites us to celebrate the bounty of the season.

You'll love this quilt for all the right reasons... color, pieced blocks, applique leaves, pumpkins and Prairie Points around the edge.

instructions on pages 40 - 41

Lone Star Pillow

pieced by Rose Ann Pegran

This prairie point bordered pillow, with its clean lines and sharp colors will blend with any home decor.

For those who love small projects, this little pillow is an opportunity to practice both your piecing and applique techniques.

instructions on page 30

SUPPLIERS

Most quilt and fabric stores carry an excellent assortment of supplies. If you need something special, ask your local store to contact the following companies.

DIE-CUTTER and DIES FOR CUTTING with AccuQuilt® GO!™ Fabric Cutter and GO! Fabric Cutting Dies AccuQuilt
www.accuquilt.com

FABRICS and Layer Cakes: Moda Fabrics
www.unitednotions.com

QUILTING BY
Susan Corbett, 817-361-7762
Julie Lawson, 817-428-5929
Sue Needle, 817-589-1168

MANY THANKS to my staff for their cheerful help and wonderful ideas!

Kathy Mason
Patty Williams
Donna Kinsey
Kristy Krouse
David & Donna Thomason

Totes on the GO!™

sewn by Donna Arends Hansen and Donna Perrotta

Your gear, the project for the guild meeting, and the embroidery you work on while waiting for the kids' music lessons all need their own bag.

It's so much easier when every project has its own tote. And now, we are even encouraged to bring our own bags to the grocery store! Make life easier with an assortment of totes for yourself and your friends today.

instructions on pages 25 - 27